THE BIRTHDAY BOYS

For Petty Officer Jan Boud
and Leading Stoker David Tomlinson

THE BIRTHDAY BOYS

Beryl Bainbridge

Carroll & Graf Publishers, Inc.
New York

Copyright © 1991 by Beryl Bainbridge

First Carroll & Graf edition April 1994
First Carroll & Graf trade paperback edition 1995

Carroll & Graf Publishers, Inc.
260 Fifth Avenue
New York, NY 10001

Library of Congress Cataloging-in-Publication Data

Bainbridge, Beryl, 1933–
    The birthday boys / Beryl Bainbridge—1st Carroll & Graf ed.
    p.   cm.
    ISBN 0-7867-0207-9 : $9.95
    1. Scott, Robert Falcon, 1868–1912—Fiction.   2. British Antarctic
("Terra Nova") Expedition (1910–1913)—Fiction.   3. South Pole—
Discovery and exploration—Fiction.   4. Explorers—Antarctic
Regions—Fiction.   5. Explorers—Great Britain—Fiction.   I. Title.
PR6052.A3195B57   1994
823'.914—dc20   94-1264
                                                                              CIP

Manufactured in the United States of America

Contents

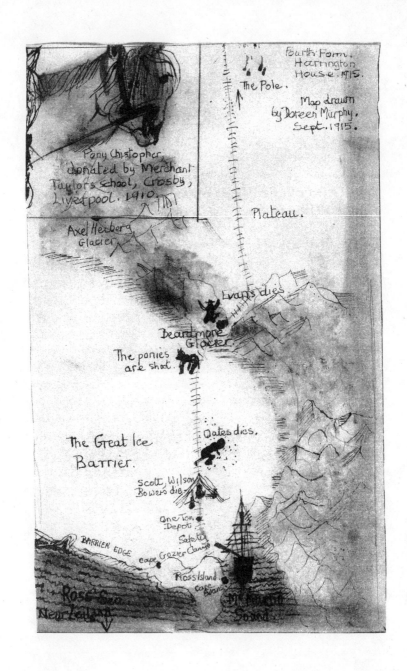

Fourth Form.
Harrington
House. 1915.

The Pole.

Map drawn
by Doreen Murphy,
Sept. 1915.

Pony Christopher
donated by Merchant
Taylor's school, Crosby,
Liverpool. 1910.

Plateau.

Axel Heiberg
Glacier

Evans dies

Beardmore
Glacier

The ponies
are shot.

The Great Ice
Barrier.

Oates dies.

Scott, Wilson
Bowers die

One Ton
Depot

Safety
Camp

BARRIER EDGE
cape Crozier
cape

Ross Island
cape Evans

Ross Sea.

New Zealand

McMurdo
Sound

Petty Officer Edgar (Taff) Evans
June 1910

We left West India Dock for Cardiff on the first day of June. None of us were sorry, least of all the Owner. For a month we'd had the dignitaries coming aboard, poking their scientific noses into everything, leaving their fingermarks on the brass work shining in the sunlight, the ladies under their parasols shuddering in mock fear as the pig-iron ballast swung overhead. 'How picturesque it all is,' they trilled. 'How thrilling.' We'd had to keep our shirts on and mind our language.

The night after I signed on I took a drop too much to drink; and the next, and the one following. I'm not proud of my behaviour, what with being on short pay and having little enough to send home to the wife, but how else is a man to fill in his nights when he's far from home and without a berth?

While the ship was undergoing refitment and the mess deck out of action, me and Tom Crean lodged with William Lashly at his auntie's house on the Isle of Dogs. Trouble is, Crean was never a man for enjoying a bevvy, and neither Will nor I felt tranquil parked by the fire of an evening with only the auntie and her tabby cat for company. Living ashore hits men differently. Some shuffle back into it like they've found an old pair of slippers and others can't walk easy, no matter how they're shod.

That being said, me and Will didn't have to put our hands in our pockets all that often; no sooner had the whisper got round that we were on the *Terra Nova* than there was always someone ready to stand us a drink in return for a yarn. Lashly can coax a sick engine into life like it was an infant far gone with the croup, but he has a brutal way with his mother-tongue. It was left to me to spin the tales. 'Tell them about the blizzard on Castle Rock,' he'd prompt. 'Tell them how Vince met his Maker,' and off I'd go.

There's a trick to holding attention, to keeping interest at full pitch, and I learnt it as a boy from Idris Williams, the preacher in the chapel at the bottom of Glamorgan Street. It's a matter of knowing which way the wind blows and of trimming sails accordingly. All the same, I've never found it necessary to alter my description of the cold, or of the ice flowers that bloomed in winter along the edges of the sea.

'It was in the March of 1902,' I'd begin, 'and the *Discovery* was anchored in McMurdo Bay under the shadow of Mount Erebus. In a few short weeks the sun would go down and fail to rise and the long winter nights set in.' I'd add a spot of detail – how we built huts for ourselves and kennels for the dogs, though the last was a bloody waste of effort seeing the animals preferred to burrow in the snow, and how we butchered seals in the scant daylight hours so as to lay up fresh meat against the scurvy. Sometimes we played football, and it was a dangerous game, slithering about on the ice. 'You know what they do to horses when they breaks a leg, don't you, boys?' I'd wait then until my listeners got over laughing.

'I dare say,' I'd continue, 'that you think you've known what it is to be cold,' and there'd be a murmur of agreement from men who had sailed the China Seas on windjammers bucking in a force twelve, the waves curling forty feet high and not a patch of clothing that didn't stick like a leech to their backs. 'But you *can't* know,' I'd say, quietly enough. 'Not until you've been south. To be cold is when the temperature sinks to −60°F and the mercury freezes in the thermometer. Petrol won't burn, see, at this degree and even an Eskimo dog can't work, because its lungs will stop functioning. Real cold is ...' and here I'd drop silent, jaw clenched, as though in the contemplation of such cold the words had frozen in my mouth. Shuddering, I'd shove my empty glass about the table. Then, after someone had placed another measure in my hand, I'd tell them, 'To be cold is when the snot freezes in your nostrils and your breath snaps like a fire-cracker on the air and falls to ice in your beard.'

I was speaking no more than the gospel truth. It had been as bad as that, and worse, when we'd gone in search of Hare, floundering about in the ghastly twilight with the blizzard roaring about our ears. The Owner had despatched us onto the Barrier to test our skill on skis and see what weights we could pull sledge-hauling. At first the weather had been in our favour. It was ten degrees below, but the going was so hard, up to our knees in drifts and pulling those damned sledges because no one knew how to work the dogs, that we were stripped down to our vests. On the sixth day a blizzard blew up, and Hare went missing. Three of us turned back to look for him. It was madness; the dogs yapping in a tangle of traces and the wind cutting our faces like knives. Vince wasn't wearing crampons, and when he slipped he had no purchase. 'He called out something as he slid past me over the cliff ... but I couldn't hear him, see, on account of the wind.'

Again I'd pause, only this time I wasn't codding, for no matter how often I told it I relived the moment, that moment between Vince being there and being gone. I kept to myself how my heart leapt in my breast with joy that it was him that was lost and not me. Nor did I think it fit to let on how badly the Owner had taken the news of Vince's death. Crean heard him blubbing in the night. Dr Wilson sat up with him, attempting to persuade him it was God's will. The Owner doesn't find it easy to delegate and he held himself responsible. There were those among us, though they'd have thought twice before voicing it in my presence, who considered this no more than just.

'The next day,' I'd conclude, 'when we'd returned safely to base camp, ice flowers had formed on the newly frozen sea, sculptured blooms like those waxen wreaths in the cemeteries of home.' And that was the truth too, give or take another week or so.

Some nights, if the men grouped around us were still sober enough to listen, I'd throw in the yarn about the Owner and me stepping into space on the Ferrar Glacier. We'd been crawling across the plateau and toiling up those bloody mountains for weeks, whipped by the wind, the sledge runners torn to shreds, laid up in blizzards so fierce that the stove wouldn't burn and we chewed half-frozen food for sustenance. Come night-time, we huddled together in a three-man sleeping bag, and to begin with me and Lashly were uneasy at sharing dossing-room with an officer, until we caught on that it was his poor warmth and ours that was keeping us all alive. Lashly was hit bad with the frostbite, his fingers swollen fat as plums.

He was leading, me and the Owner hauling behind,

when we dropped into the crevasse. The sledge we were dragging catapulted into the air and jammed bridge-like above us, and we dangled there between blue walls of ice, close as sweethearts, facing death and each other. The damnest thing, in spite of the cold I got a hard on. I suspect it was the best of me, rising up in protest against extinction. I was scared for my life, but at the same time I couldn't help noticing how bright everything was, the ice not really blue at all but shot through with spangled points of rosy light so dazzling that it made me crinkle up my eyes as though I had something to smile about, and there was a shadow cast by the Owner's shoulder that washed from seagreen to purple as he twisted in his traces. He hung a foot or so above, and when I looked up at his face I'd never seen such anxiety in a man's eyes, and it was for me, not him. All at once he let out a sigh, as though until then he hadn't been breathing, and he said, 'Are you all right, Taff?' and I said, polite enough, 'Don't trouble yourself about me, sir.'

There were any number of words roaring through my head, but when we were out of our pickle at last and lay spreadeagled on the ice, I came up with nothing better than, 'Well, I'm blowed.' Mostly I told the story as it happened, only generally I left out the bit about the sweethearts.

Later, we'd have a few more drinks and continue fairly matey until a carelessly expressed remark by some dog of a merchant seaman would send us out into the alley-way for a scrap, after which, if Crean is to be believed, we rolled home and burst all but insensible through the yard door, bellowing of pursuit by demons. I expect lost Vince ran at our heels.

It was Tom Crean who first alerted me that the Owner was thinking of going south again. He was coxswain on the battleship *Bulwark*, then under the command of the Owner, when the news came through that Shackleton had turned back only half a dozen marches short of the Pole. 'I think we should have a shot at it, don't you, Tom?' the Owner said, and Tom said, 'Yes, sir, I think we should.'

I didn't rush. After the way I'd acquitted myself on the previous jaunt I reckoned my application for inclusion in this present one was in the nature of a formality. And I was right.

'What delayed you, Taff?' the Owner asked, tongue-in-cheek, when I went down to London and presented myself at his offices in Victoria Street.

'I didn't think it was a matter of urgency, sir,' I replied, and was careful to smile with the right amount of deference. The Owner can be a stickler for what passes for the right attitude.

'I'm glad to have you with me, Evans,' he said. 'It wouldn't be the same without you.'

The roistering nights ended soon enough. The crew having mustered and the shipwright allowing us aboard, we slung our hammocks where we could and came under the authority of the Mate. Crean holds it's like old *Discovery* times, him and me and Lashly together again along with the Owner and Dr Wilson. I don't mind the doctor, though it's not easy to engage him in conversation, not unless you're knowledgeable about birds and their eggs. He being a serious sort of cove, lacking the common touch for all he believes to the contrary, and religious into the bargain, I can't help thinking less of him than the Owner. Both of them come from what the privileged classes assume to be humble backgrounds, meaning that from guilt, temperament or the ill winds blown up by life's vicissitudes

12

they've felt compelled to earn a living. I'm not up on the Doctor's family, but I do know that two of the Owner's sisters are dressmakers and a third went on the stage, albeit not in the capacity of a dancer or a feed in a vaudeville act. I've come to the conclusion the Doctor pursues his chosen course on account of spiritual leanings, whereas the Owner's driven by necessity.

I don't want there to be misconceptions; more than most I'm in a position to evaluate the Doctor's worth, and even a cynic would have to admit he's not just a Sunday Christian. You could label him a peacemaker. On more than one occasion during the expedition of 1901 he took the Owner aside and told him a few home-truths. There was a lot of bad feeling between the Owner and Shackleton, and it was causing discord all round. The Owner has a bit of a temper, see, and when things go wrong he's apt to sound off. It's not that he lacks control, rather that he's nervy, and who can blame him when he's burdened with such heavy responsibilities? There's no doubt he relies on the Doctor to keep him serene and treading water. He calls him Uncle Bill, although Wilson's the younger of the two.

The ward-room have taken quite a shine to a newcomer called Bowers shipped hot-foot from Bombay, a former cadet on the *Worcester* and now seconded from the Royal India Marine with the rank of lieutenant. He's a rum little bugger with short legs, sandy hair and a nose shaped like a parrot's – the officers have already nicknamed him 'Birdie' – and on first clapping eyes on him the Owner is supposed to have said, 'Well, we're landed with him and must make the best of it.' Crean says he had to be accepted because he came highly recommended from Sir Clements Markham.

Within half an hour of stowing his kit Bowers stepped backwards and fell nineteen feet into the hold. I peered down at his face, red on arrival and now dark in shadow, his barrel chest unaccountably heaving up and down, and remarked, 'He's breathing, lads, but he's a gonner.' We all thought he'd broken his back on the pig-iron, but ten seconds later he bounced up unscathed.

Since then, the Owner refers to him as a perfect treasure, and although I won't go so far overboard I will concede he's a worker and strong as they come. Lashly maintains he may well turn out to be the toughest of us all. 'Why is that?' I asked him, and he said it was owing to his being so bloody ugly. 'A man like that,' he said, 'has a need to prove himself.'

The Owner admires physical strength above most things; I suspect it has something to do with him being considered sickly as a child. By that I don't mean to imply he was ailing, rather that he lacked robustness, languished under a melancholy disposition. It's been my experience that men overburdened with emotions often have an exaggerated regard for muscle. I don't let on I'm sentimental myself by nature; that's why him and me get on so well. To my knowledge he's never flinched from a show of feeling exhibited by his equals, but I reckon he'd be discomfited if I went in for the same sort of caper; being down a crevasse together is no excuse for stepping out of line. All I know is I'd die with the man, and for him, God help me, if the necessity arose.

There's another bloke arrived from India, a Captain Oates of the Fifth Royal Inniskilling Dragoons. He presented himself on the dock wearing an ancient raincoat and an old bowler-hat. None of us knew what to make of him, and some took him for a farmer. Crean says he's paid a thousand pounds to join the expedition and that he's down on the parole for a shilling a month. I'd have known he had money without being told, just by the easy way he conducts himself and his disregard of appearances. The talk is that he distinguished himself fighting the Boers and lay in a dried-up river-bed east of Kaarkstroom with a bullet through him. He's been taken on because he's an authority on horseflesh, and it had been planned he travel out to Siberia to join Mr Meares and advise on what ponies to buy, only he quickly became such a favourite, such a willing dogsbody, that the mate begged the Owner to keep him aboard. The other day he returned from being ashore, looking more dishevelled than usual. Everyone had been ordered to the dental surgeon that afternoon, and I asked him if he'd had a rough time in the chair.

'I didn't go,' he said. 'I borrowed a friend's motor-bike instead and took a spin as far as Greenwich.'

'Well, now sir,' I said, 'was that wise? The cold can play the very devil with a man's mouth.' I should know, seeing I lost most of the nerves in my lower jaw at Cape Crozier, and my teeth along with them.

'I'm against medical precautions,' he said. 'There's an awful lot of rot talked about germs. In India one was almost forced at gunpoint to be vaccinated against smallpox. I refused.'

'You were very lucky to get away with it then sir,' I said.

'I didn't,' he replied. 'I went down with it in Bombay and damn near died.'

He's pleasant with me, no side to him at all, yet I sense a space around him. He has a manner of eyeing people, even if he's standing face to face, as though he sees them from a distance.

The only foul-weather Jack among the officers, thus far, is my namesake, Lieutenant 'Teddy' bloody Evans. He's going to be in command of the ship until we reach Capetown, the Owner being obliged to stay behind to pay off bills and drum up more money. Though I'll allow Lt. Evans is a capable enough seaman, it's my opinion he suffers under illusions of grandeur. On the strength of having influential connections in Cardiff, he's been raising funds for the expedition by poncing up and down the country waxing poetic on the Land of his Fathers – and him with about as much Welsh blood in his veins as the Kaiser. Besides, he has a down on me on account of the drinking, which is rich when you think of the kerfuffle he raises of an evening after they've passed round the port in the wardroom.

The day before last I was working up near the forecastle with Lt. Bowers. He's responsible for the stores – food, paraffin, excess clothing and suchlike – and I'm officer in charge of the scientific and polar journey equipment. It's not up to me to say whose job is the more important. God help us if we made landfall only to find the sledge runners defective, the lamps without wicks and the sleeping-bags unlined; but then, I doubt if any of these items, in apple-pie order or otherwise, would be of much use if we were lacking the necessities of life. I was just shifting a crate of whisky, donated by some distillery in the Midlands, in order to get at a consignment of photographic chemicals, when Lt. Evans came up and said, 'Well, now, Petty Officer, I see you're giving due consideration to the priorities.'

Thing is, I had a black eye. From the way he looked at me a blind moggie could tell he thought I'd come by it in a brawl. 'Yes, sir,' I said, controlled enough. The worst thing a man can do is to belittle another. The next worse thing is for a man to make the mistake of justifying himself.

'I'm keeping my eye on you, Taff,' he said, but smiling, as if he was jocularly referring to my shiner.

'That's what's needed in this job, sir,' I replied, which was a dig at him, and I trust it went home. Originally, see, he'd been in charge of equipment, until I spotted something wrong with the skis newly arrived from Norway and informed the Owner directly, whereupon he ordered the Lieutenant to hand the whole caboodle over to me.

Lt. Bowers kept his head down all the while. Had he been older he might have said something in my defence, having been present the night before when one of the crew tripped coming down the companion-way and jabbed the bridge of my nose with his elbow. Once Lt. Evans was out of earshot, he said, 'It's unfair, but a man's reputation often goes before him.'

Brooding on it since, I should have spoken up. If I'm the pisspot they take me for, how do they think I held down the post of gymnastics instructor, let alone won the Naval Tattoo competition for field gunnery two years running?

Crean, who overheard Dr. Wilson remarking that 'Teddy was a cheerful soul, but something of a Peter Pan', advises me I should keep my head low and bide my time. Rumour has it that Evans was intent on leading an expedition of his own, only he didn't have the backing of the Geographical Society. For this presumption the Owner's none to warm towards him and won't be long in finding he lacks ballast.

We've had our work cut out preparing the *Terra Nova* for sea. She's an old Dundee whaling ship built in 1884 – the Owner had set his heart on getting hold of the

Discovery again but the Hudson Bay Company wouldn't part with her.

First thing, when the *Nova* limped into dock, was to get rid of her blubber tanks. The stench of seal oil was enough to make a sewer-rat heave. When Davies, the shipwright, first took a gander at her he pronounced her little short of a wreck, fit only for the knacker's yard. He was looking on the dark side. True, if you peer too closely you can still spot the tell-tale strengthening pieces in her cross-trees and detect the furrows worn in her sides where she's been ground by ice-floes, but she's sweet enough now she's been white-washed and her bilges swilled out, and sound where it counts.

It's been more a matter of alteration than repair. She's barque-rigged and fitted to the requirements of the Expedition, with laboratories built on the poop for the scientists, a dark-room for the photographer, a new stove in the galley, instrument and chronometer-rooms, an ice-house for the frozen meat, on top of which, owing to it being free of iron, we've stuck the standard compass and the pedestal needed for magnetic work.

The amount of stuff we've managed to pack in beggars description, and there's next to no pilfering going on. Half the items – tobacco, cigars, fancy chocolates, crystallised fruits, curried meat in tins, Christmas puddings, baked beans, even a pianola – have been given for nothing, and the crew seem to take this for a sign of generosity. I could spell out to them the increased profits likely to accrue to Messrs. Burroughs and Wellcome when it becomes known they're suppliers of photographic equipment to Mr Ponting of the Polar Expedition, not to mention the rush on sales when the Wolsey Underwear Company advertise their wind-proof drawers as those worn by the southern explorers, but it strikes me as prudent to keep my mouth shut. I've known ships so rife with thieving that the only thing likely to remain in place was the galley stove, and that because it was too hot to handle.

The Owner's paid £100 out of expedition funds to have the *Terra Nova* registered as a yacht. This enables us to fly the White Ensign; more to the point, it means we can dodge the attentions of Board of Trade officials who would most certainly declare her an ill-founded ship within the meaning of the Act, seeing she's wallowing so low in the water it was a waste of time to smudge out the Plimsoll line. Fresh painted lamp-black, with a funnel yellow as a buttercup and a neat white line all round her bows, she's now as pretty as a picture. There's one thing worries Lashly: she's going to be the very devil when it comes to consuming coal.

*

Before we sailed from West India Dock the wife of the First Sea Lord broke the White Ensign from our masthead. Every ship for miles around set off their hooters as we moved out into the river. A huge crowd had gathered to wish us godspeed; they ran in a tide along the dock, hats raised, a blizzard of handkerchieves fluttering farewell. We had known in our minds all along we were leaving, but it was only now that we knew it in our hearts, and more than one of us dashed the tears from his eyes. Mr Ponting, the photographer, observed to the Owner that if this was our departure, what on earth would our homecoming be like? The Owner was less enthusiastic, he said he didn't care for this sort of fuss, that all he wanted was to finish the work begun on the *Discovery* and get back to the Navy. I don't think he altogether approves of Mr Ponting, suspecting him of being tainted by commercialism. The word is that Mr Ponting's struck a hard bargain in regards to copyright and such matters.

We took nine days to reach Cardiff, making stops all along the Channel to acknowledge money given and in hopes of receiving more. Sir Clements Markham and party came with us, and the Owner's wife. Mrs Scott's a handsome woman and confident with it. On boarding, she strolled up to Captain Oates and says, cool as you please, 'I see you're wearing laces in your boots today, Captain Oates.' He fairly wriggled. I noticed the Owner looking at her once or twice as if he wasn't sure what she might do next.

First stop was at Greenhithe, where we dropped anchor off the training ship *Worcester*. The Owner disembarked soon after to pick up two flags donated by Queen Alexandra, one to be brought back, suitably weather-worn, and one to be hoisted furthest south. At this rate we'll have more flags than sails. Before he went ashore he addressed the cadets and told them he had no objection to their looking over the *Terra Nova*. Mrs Scott waved to me as she left.

She's taller than the Owner and it's not just on account of her hat, because I've seen her without one, the afternoon he sent me round to his house to collect a document he'd forgotten. She wears her hair down indoors and goes barefoot. On that occasion, she said, 'So you're Petty Officer Evans. Con often refers to you as a gentle giant', Con being a diminutive of Falcon, the Owner's second name. I blushed. She's ladylike but her manner and gaze are very direct.

They don't live in any great style. I noticed they were short on carpets and had just a few rugs strewn about the floor, and though I can't swear to it I reckon the sofa, judging by its list to starboard, was missing a leg. She asked if I wanted to take a peek at the baby, and when I said I did she took me out into the garden at the back. He was in his pram with the hood pushed down and a stiff wind blowing. 'There's nothing more likely to make a child thrive,' she said, 'than fresh air. And love, of course.'

When I told the wife about the air she flared up and said it was all right for some, that if we put our little one out in the backyard he'd be dead in a week, what with the sulphurous fumes from the tin-plate works and enough soot coming down over Swansea to make him into a piccaninny.

With the Owner gone, Lt. Evans was in his element. He'd done his training on the *Worcester* and it evidently gave him no end of satisfaction to return as Master of such a celebrated vessel, even if she is nothing more than a whaler masquerading as a yacht. He turned to me some time during the afternoon, a crocodile of youthful wide-eyed lads slithering in his wake, and exclaimed, '*Dewch*, it's wonderful to be off at last, isn't it, Taff?' He used the Welsh as though it came natural to him.

'*Dewch*, that it is, indeed to goodness, sir,' I replied, but the irony skimmed past him like a feather on the breeze. His eyes had a boy's light in them, guileless, shiny with hope, and I was sorry afterwards I'd made sarcastic with him. When we get back he'll become a Captain for real, and then he'll be down on the list in line for an Admiral. To each his own dream, and I know mine.

It was the lack of space, the smell of clothes drying in front of the fire, that set my mind on the sea. The first thing the wife does, when she knows I'm due for a spell of coming ashore, is to get rid of the washing and park the umbrella-stand against the front door to keep it wide open. I grew fast, and big, and the bigger I got the pokier our Mam's house became, not a chair easy enough for me to sit in, nor a bed long enough to lie on. I cracked my head on the lintel of the door every time I went out back to the privvy. Most times I felt like a fish in a net. I was young then, and sailing the oceans let me stretch my limbs and expand my lungs.

I'm slowing down now, I can't deny it, and when I return I ought to be in a position to quit the sea and buy a little pub in Cardigan Bay. I stayed there once as a boy in my Mam's brother's house near Criccieth. His wasn't a big house either, but there was a meadow alongside and an orchard beyond with a view of sands the colour of milk on the turn. In the right season my aunty kept a copper perched on a fire above a cattle grid in the orchard, and there was so much fruit to cook we stayed up all night feeding the flames with sticks. We baked bruised apples in the embers and juggled them in our palms until they were cool enough to eat. In the morning the whole world smelt of jam.

I've tried to make my wife glimpse the silver lining, painted word-pictures of sunsets and sunrises free of smoke, of columbine snaking along a garden wall, of the baby's cheeks tinted pink as an albertine in bloom, but she's a pessimist and all she talks about is setbacks, death, an inadequate widow's pension and her and the children thrown on the parish. All the same, I notice she never wastes an opportunity to boast of where I'm headed.

The 3rd of June found us off Spithead, where the Superintendent of Compasses came on board and swung the ship. I was fretting the Owner mightn't get back for his birthday but he turned up on the 4th. I'd bought him a little gift of two Havanas and a card with a picture of Nelson on the front. We've got 3,500 cigars in the hold already, and I wouldn't like him to think I hadn't paid for his out of my own pocket. I presented my offering on the morning of the 6th, finding him temporarily on his own in the wardroom.

He was sitting in his chair at the head of the table, scribbling across a pile of papers.

'A token of my esteem, sir,' I said. 'Many happy returns.'

'How very kind of you, Evans,' he said. 'I'm much obliged to you', and he put the package unopened into his pocket and continued with his writing. I don't know what I expected, a handshake perhaps, a tot in celebration of his birth date – an offer which I would have refused, unless pressed. At any rate, I was left feeling flat.

That evening, after completing a series of magnetic observations in the Solent, Lt. Evans announced we were welcome on board the *Invincible* which was anchored nearby. 'It goes without saying,' he said, 'that I expect you to conduct yourselves like gentlemen.' Come ten o'clock we could hear the racket the officers were making at table clear over the ship, and him in particular. One of his party tricks is to pick a man up in his teeth by the seat of the trousers.

I don't recall much of the latter part of the evening, beyond we were presented with two sledges and that at midnight me, Lashly and Crean were detailed by Mr Campbell, the mate, to stow a load of canvas in the boat and row with muffled oars to the *Terra Nova*. After which the Owner called me up from the lower deck to have a word.

'I'm leaving now, Petty Officer,' he said. 'I'll see you in Portsmouth.'

'Right you are, sir,' I replied. 'Portsmouth it is.'

'Do you know what I'm going to do?' he asked me. 'Before I leave England?'

'Make a will, sir,' I said, quick as a flash.

'Near,' he said, smiling. 'I'm going home to carve my initials on a tree that I've planted, and when I've done so I shall sit under it and smoke one of your excellent cigars.'

As it happened, my talk of wills wasn't short of the mark. He rejoined us on the 8th, a day of thick fog. We were taken in tow to the Needles and then to Weymouth Bay where the Home Fleet of the new *Dreadnought* class had assembled to pay its respects. We moved between those monstrous ships like a tiddler among whales. The time can't be far off when the strength of a man's arm, his knowledge of tides, of winds, will count for nothing, and I, for one, am glad I'll be beached by then. When we were under the muzzles of the *Dreadnought* guns we held our breath. I daresay the mist added to our sense of awe; how else, but in silence, could one bob past the jaws of hell.

We rounded Portland Bill at sunset, and a short while later the Owner ordered the men aft and said it was his wish that every man should make a will. He would, he said, give advice as to the allotting of money. We smirked inwardly, most of us having nothing to leave but debts, and the rest about as much as could be tied up in a handkerchief.

While the Owner was talking, Lt. Evans had cause to ease the *Terra Nova* down, take soundings and go full astern to avoid our being in collision with a steamer; the Owner's voice shook and he coughed to hide it. As

Lashly put it, we'd have looked a right bunch of knuckle-heads if we'd sunk in home waters.

On the 11th of June we weighed anchor in the Cardiff Roads and the Pilot came aboard to steer us into Roath Dock to berth alongside the bunting-decked warehouses of the Crown Patent Fuel Company. No businessman ever gives something without wanting a return. The Crown Company was supplying us free of charge with three-hundred tons of compressed briquettes of coal and bitumen, for which largesse the Owner had to smarm his way through the attentions of yet another welcoming party. He's good at that sort of thing when he concentrates his mind; he has only to smile to set the ladies fluttering, but you can tell he finds it a strain by the way he keeps glancing over his shoulder to reassure himself Dr Wilson is at hand.

The coaling of the ship was completed that same afternoon under his supervision. He didn't have to be there, but I reckon he found it preferable to spending time hobnobbing with the company directors and their wives. When it was over all hands were landed for the ship to be fumigated and blown free of coal dust, after which we were invited – compliments of the management – to the second house of the Empire Theatre Music Hall. The Owner went hotfoot back to London.

The same tedious procedure of loading and cleansing happened all over again on the Saturday, following our removal to the Bute Dock to take on board a hundred tons of steam coal. It was then that the shipwrights' original misgivings came home to roost. The *Terra Nova* settled dangerously low in the water and leakage occurred in the bows. We all had to heave to, caulking and cementing the timbers. Lt. Evans warned us to keep our mouths shut in case word got round and we were prevented from leaving on time. Lashly thinks the trouble stems from the renewal-plates put in to strengthen the ship for the icepack; some bloody dock-worker has used the wrong-sized rivets.

Saturday night we were given shore leave, and I went to the house of my brother-in-law Hugh Price to join my wife Lois who had travelled up from Rhosili to say goodbye. My mother had come too, and her brother David Williams from Criccieth, now an old man, and so far gone in the head as not to know the time of day any more. It was an ordeal my mother being there, crying over me and carrying on as though our next meeting was destined to take place beyond the bright blue sky, forcing me to divide my attention between her and Lois and the baby. What with my brother-in-law's three grown lads living at home and the neighbours popping in and out to shake me by the hand, it wasn't long before I wished I was back on board. However delicately put, there's always one question nobody can wait to ask, namely how does a man perform his bodily functions in a temperature below zero. You can hold yourself in your hands, I tell them, when you're passing water, but when it's a matter of something more pressing, no matter how you position yourself, it's a frost-bitten bum for sure. I was beating about the bush, for that isn't quite the way of it. There were times in the *Discovery* days when we did our business in our britches and shook out the turds when they froze.

A bit of a storm blew up between me and the wife. She was pestering to know how my pay was going to come through. I could only tell her she had no need to bother her head for the next six months – after that it was a question of working out what remained in the Expedition kitty. 'You can rest easy,' I said. 'The Owner has given his word that the families won't do without.'

'What use will a word be to me,' she flared up, 'when you and your precious Owner are thousands of miles away playing at snowmen?'

The brother-in-law didn't improve the situation. 'I seen a photograph of Captain Scott's wife in the newspaper this morning,' he said. 'You told me she was a good-looking woman, and by God, she is.'

'I don't know that I expressed an opinion one way or the other,' I said.

'Yes, you did,' he insisted.

'I was talking about his mother, see,' I said. 'The Captain's very attached to his mother.'

The damn fool wouldn't let it go. My Mam compounded it by nudging my uncle and shouting into his ear that I thought the world of Captain Scott. It beats me why she had to bring the uncle into it; judging by the baffled look in his drowned eyes he was having difficulty in fathoming who I was, never mind the Owner.

'Not the world,' I protested, attempting to get hold of my wife's hand under the table, only to have her snatch it from my grasp as if she'd touched dirt. I felt I was being torn in all directions, so much so that when Hugh Price suggested we go off to the pub I jumped at it. It wasn't as though my wife was hanging on my every word and putting herself out to make a fuss of me. On the contrary, she was looking daggers all the while I was eating my tea.

There was a fellow in the pub who came straight up and wanted to know if it was true that the *Terra Nova* was unseaworthy. 'What gave you that idea?' I asked. 'I read it in the newspaper,' he said. 'It says they're having to use the pumps.' I saw him off with a flea in his ear, but later the brother-in-law was daft enough to repeat what had been said in front of my mother, which set her weeping again.

I was all for going straight off to my bed, it being the last night me and Lois would snuggle down together for three long years, but she said she had to give the baby its feed and she didn't want me lumbering about while she was trying to get him winded.

Hugh Price fetched the cards from the sideboard. The old uncle was laid out on the sofa; every time the coals settled, or one of us swore or thumped the table, he shouted, 'Is that you knocking, Lizzie ... is that you, *cariad?*' and we shouted back, 'Hush there, Lizzie's long since gone to her bed', which was no more than an arrangement of the truth, seeing his wife Elizabeth had been unravelling in the ground for the last twenty years. Once, when next door booted the cat out for the night and it let off a yowl, he sat bolt upright and exclaimed, 'Keep still, you bugger, I haven't finished yet.'

I slept badly. There's a gas-lamp directly outside the window and it casts a glow, never quite still, on a patch of wallpaper above the wardrobe. In my fanciful state it seemed the wall was shifting. Some time in the small hours the clock on the landing stopped and the silence swelled up louder than the ticking. I thought of how in the morning Hugh Price would start it going once more, and how when my heart ceased to beat it would be for ever, there not being a key invented that could wind me up again. Then I dwelt on all the bad things I'd done – the untruths told, the tom-catting around, the squandering of money, the filching of those two cigars with their two little labels tossed over the side – and there was the usual melancholy pleasure to the exercise. Such moral reflections are customary before a long voyage; I expect it's nature's way of preparing one for the efforts to come. A man can't give of his best if he's beset with worries of things left undone, words gone unspoken.

Lying there, I tried to go along with the notion that I was a weak and miserable sinner, and yet I had only to stretch out my arm, fist clenched huge against the lamplight, to know how strong I was, how endurable. For one dangerous moment I played with the idea of waking my wife and making a confession of sorts, just so I could go off purged, shiny as a new pin. I think the last bit of nonsense was occasioned by the tune of 'Onward Christian Soldiers' suddenly popping into my head. It's the Owner's favourite hymn, and he used to whistle it, or leastways make the attempt, when we were trying to light the primus on the glacier. His lips were so cracked with the cold he could only manage one note in ten and he sounded like a cuckoo in spring.

Thinking about it made me snort with laughter, loud enough for my wife to stir in her sleep. Earlier, she'd let me love her, albeit grudgingly. She complained my breath stank. It never ceases to puzzle me, that, while men and women's bodies fit jigsaw-tight in an altogether miraculous way their minds remain wretchedly unaligned.

I must have dozed off in the end, for the next day my wife said she'd had to clamp her hand over my mouth because I was bellowing out some name and she was feared I'd wake the baby.

'What name?' I asked, risking putting the fat on the fire. There's a woman I bumped across in San Francisco who stays in the mind, half-Indian, half-white.

'It sounded like Jesus,' my wife said, and added, 'Knowing you, it might have been Jeannie.'

I saw her and my mother off on the midday train back to Swansea. I'd told them I was expected back on board at dinner-time, though strictly speaking I wasn't required to show myself until sundown. I wanted the farewells over and done with, which was why I wasn't very chatty at the station. I tried to be lovey-dovey; indeed I felt loving, yet they sensed I was holding myself separate. It's hard to explain, but when a man's within sight of sailing it's as though he's already gone, and the distance between him and those he's leaving behind widens by the moment.

My mother took hold of the baby and shooed me and Lois further down the platform, so we could be on our own for the last few minutes. It wasn't a great success. My photograph's been in all the newspapers and people kept coming up and wanting to pat me on the back. There was a man there with a dog no bigger than a mangy rabbit, and when it sniffed round my trousers and I cuffed it with my boot he said, 'I expect you need all the practice you can get before you start marching with those huskies.'

I couldn't help laughing. A sledge-dog is part wolf, see, and will bite you to the bone as soon as look at you, and his poor brute had about as much life in it as the fur tippet my Mam drapes round her neck when she goes to chapel. My wife stalked off; I expect she thought I was laughing because I was cheerful. Then the train puffed in. My mother sat like a stone in the carriage, staring at me through the glass, the baby's head, bald as an egg, bright against the dark nest of her shoulder. Just as the train began to move Lois bunched her fingers to her lips to blow me a kiss. Then I did feel choked. Tears pricked my eyes; my mother looked so old and my wife so young.

*

30

The leakages in the *Terra Nova* were serious. By the Monday we were manning the pumps four hours out of twelve. One of the stokers, a Belgian who went under the nickname of Van Winkle, moaned that in her present condition she wasn't fit to sail, that she'd never make Madeira, never mind Capetown, and we ought to delay passage until things could be put shipshape. He was partially in the right of it, of course, even if he is a foreigner. Given favourable winds we won't fare too badly, but if we have to get up steam it will mean even longer at the pumps.

Lashly and me did our best to put the Belgian right, spelling out the urgency of establishing a base before the Antarctic winter set in – being ignorant of the South he continued to belly-ache, so much so I offered to pitch him overboard. At that, dear old Tom Crean, warm-hearted as always, took me aside and told me the man had domestic problems to contend with. 'Who hasn't, boyo?' I said, but I took his point.

I felt uneasy in myself. Monday night, the ship's company, wives included, were to muster as guests of the Cardiff Chamber of Commerce, the officers at a seven-and-sixpenny dinner at the Royal and the rest of us at a half-a-crown-do further down the road at Barry's Hotel. I had mentioned it to Lois, who'd argued she'd best get back home to look after our eldest child. It bothered me, what with our parting under a misunderstanding, that I hadn't insisted. My Mam could have looked after the kiddies.

I had the opportunity to ask Lt. Bowers if he was going to be accompanied, and he said he didn't suppose so. We were still taking aboard equipment and stores and he was in his element, knee-deep amid crates of Stone's Ginger Wine, his cap tipped to the back of his

head, writing little entries in his notebook. Mr
Cherry-Garrard was assisting him. The latter's a nice
enough young fellow, very anxious to please and make
himself liked, and halfway to it seeing he doesn't mind
putting his hand to the muckiest jobs. He has a way of
looking at you as if expecting to be struck by a fist, and
might welcome it, if only to prove he won't stagger.

'I've already been home to say goodbye to my people,'
Lt. Bowers said. 'My mother's none too keen on my
going as it is, so I see no call to drag her all this way just
so she can weep on the quayside.'

'My sentiments exactly, sir,' I said. 'It does no good to
prolong the misery.'

He proceeded to tell me how his sisters had knitted
him a woolly jumper, and what a perfectly grand time
he'd had jumping into the sea off a promontory in his
back garden. He said he loved swimming and didn't I
find it the best sport in the world? 'Captain Oates,' he
said, 'lucky devil, is thinking of putting in a pool on his
estate down in Essex ... when he returns, that is. Don't
you think that a capital idea?'

'Yes, sir,' I said, with as much enthusiasm as I could
feign, for to tell the truth I'd consider myself a lucky
devil if I could scrub the dirt off in something larger
than a tin bath in front of the fire, never mind own a
stretch of water in which to play at fishes.

I waylaid the Owner first chance I got. 'It's like this,
sir,' I said, coming straight out with it. 'Begging your
pardon, sir, but I'm worried as to arrangements for the
wages.'

'The men's pay will come through the ordinary
channels,' he said. He sounded irritated. 'I thought I
made that clear.'

So he had, but then, he'd also made it clear he was

relying on public donations and by all accounts they weren't as forthcoming as expected. I hated pestering him. He has very blue eyes, full of candour, and though they looked tired there was still an expression of concern in them, otherwise I wouldn't have pushed him. 'It's not me that's troubled, sir,' I said. 'It's the wife.'

'Then she's no cause to be,' he snapped, more vexed than ever.

'Right you are, sir,' I said. 'Thank you, sir', and walked off. I knew he'd come after me.

'Look here,' he called out. 'Would it help if I wrote to Mrs Evans? Would it alleviate matters?'

'That it would, sir,' I replied. 'I'd be much obliged.'

The Owner's shot through with gold; I trust him absolutely. There are some who might suppose the scrawling of a letter to be of little moment in the circumstances. I know differently. He has a thousand and one things to see to, and a mind so burdened with details and mathematical equations that a lesser man would sink under the weight. I daresay he wrote to Lois within the hour.

Thus relieved, I was able to look forward to the evening. A party of us, including the Belgian, got togged up early, boots and buttons glittering like glass, and swaggered down town to the posh area around St Mary's Street. We were treated like royalty every pub we entered. In the Prince Albert there was a photograph, taken by Mr Ponting, of the entire ship's company lined up against the side of the *Terra Nova*. Being so large I was right at the back of the picture, but in the Caernarvon Castle there was one of me on my own, kneeling on deck examining one of the tents. The ship's cat was sitting alongside, which gave it extra appeal.

Crean said he wouldn't be surprised if it got imprinted on the top of a biscuit tin, only they'd need to blot me out. The Duke of York, jumping the gun, had a damn big banner slung across the outside, advertising it as a drinking haunt of the southern explorers. The beer was on the house.

It's a heady feeling, being famous, and that before we've even taken a step. I'm not the only one among us – those of us, that is, who are in with a chance – who speculate inwardly as to whether we'll be on that final march to plant the flag. Among the lower ranks I reckon my only rival is Lashly, seeing Crean isn't the sort of bloke to push himself into the limelight. Like me, Lashly's big and has the added advantage of being one of the mechanics in charge of the motorised sledges, which means he'll be useful right up to the last slog. They'll want someone from the ranks, mark my words, so as to avoid the accusation of nepotism. I don't doubt there'll be photographs at the end too, with the dear old Union Jack flapping away in the background.

Lashly got embroiled in an argument in the Duke of York with Van Winkle. I overheard most of it, because I had an ear cocked in case the Belgian sounded off about the leaks. It had something to do with a lack of truth in daily life and people taking a drop too much and consequently slacking at their duties. Van Winkle said, 'The neglect is there for all to see', and Lashly replied scornfully – or so I thought at the time – 'It must be a burden, you being here while it's going on', at which I flailed out, more clumsily than in anger, biffing the Belgian on the mouth and shouting he was talking from his backside.

I was defending Lashly as much as myself. He's not a boozer, see, and never could be, though it's more out of fear than conviction. As for me, I drink when I'm among those with a thirst on – how else can a man slide out of himself and shine in the general chat? For my pains, Lashly called me a bloody fool and removed himself to another table to sit with the ship's cook.

Later, I went off to the gents and there was Van Winkle crouched on the tiles with his arms cradled over his head. A fly was buzzing about his ears and he let it come to rest on his fingers, which is always the sign of a broken man. 'Don't be a soft beggar,' I said. 'I didn't hurt you.'

'Would that you could,' he replied, or words to that effect.

'What's that supposed to mean?' I asked, and he moaned, 'It's only her who has the power to wound me.'

It turns out he's strapped to a wife who's taken to the bottle after becoming enamoured of a clerk in the offices of a diamond merchant. The Belgian's mother has written telling him the wife's gadding out every night, leaving the kiddies to fend for themselves.

'Get up,' I said, feeling bad, and I hoisted him to his feet and helped wash the rusting blood from his mouth. 'Jump ship,' I advised. 'Where we're going the cold will snap you in two if your heart isn't whole.'

I was speaking hard sense. To make a miscalculation in the selection of provisions is serious enough; to pick the wrong man when there's a lengthy voyage ahead is inviting disaster. It's the old business of the rotten apple in the barrel. We all lean towards contamination. I had nothing against the Belgian; indeed I was sorry for him, and I daresay given an advantageous turn in the weather he would have tacked safe home. As things stood, I have no guilt about my subsequent interference, him in his present volatile state being every bit as dangerous as a spark in the vicinity of a powder-keg.

The Barry Hotel served up a good dinner of leek soup, with lamb cutlets to follow and a fair amount of beer. They had a Boys' Brigade band going oompah-pah on the rostrum at the end of the room, and a menu with a picture of the *Terra Nova* embossed across the top with the words *Sailed from Cardiff, June 1910* printed underneath. I thought I'd folded it away to send home to Lois, but when I turned out my pockets the next day all I could find was a cigar butt and two pudding spoons encrusted with custard.

Those who had brought wives, or were courting, had a jollier time of it than the rest of us, spaced as we were between sundry tradesmen and their ladies. The couples got to their feet and waltzed about the floor, larking and smooching, while we unfortunates were left to indulge in conversation. I'm no fool. Having been exposed to persons of the calibre of the Owner, I know a forever gentleman when I fall over him, as compared to a temporary one, and though our hosts were kind enough and more than anxious to do us proud, most of them, beyond having money in the bank, were no better than I am.

There was a chap seated at my right hand who was employed in some lowly capacity by the Crown Patent Fuel Company. He would keep asking me to put a figure to the value of the briquettes they'd given us. I knew to the last penny, but I played the game and made out they must have cost twice as much. This tickled him no end and he left his seat and went up and down the table recounting what I'd said, at which a little fellow in pince-nez thumped the cloth with his fist and challenged me to estimate the worth of his particular contribution of galley pans and cutlery. I was just making signals to Crean, jerking my head in the direction of the door and indicating we should make a run for it, when a red-faced individual in a dicky and a frock-coat bustled up the steps onto the rostrum, and flapped his hand for the conductor to lower his baton.

'The Lord Mayor of Cardiff,' he announced, 'would be obliged if the crew of the *Terra Nova* would adjourn to the Royal Hotel and join with Captain Scott and members of the Chamber of Commerce at a smoking concert.'

We walked in crocodile to the hotel, the chap in the dicky marching at our head like a drum-major. People in the street cheered and raised their hats as we passed by. Just as we filed alongside the doors of the Mercantile Insurance offices a pigeon dropped its mess on the shoulder of our leader. He wasn't aware of it and mistook the roar of laughter for high spirits. Some of the men doubled off down a side street to the nearest pub, but there was no way I was going to let the Owner down. He hates all the formal palaver, and I expect it was at his suggestion that we were fetched.

He and his wife, along with Lt. Evans and his missus, have been staying at the Mansion House as guests of the Lord Mayor. Though no doubt the Lieutenant has enjoyed himself to the hilt, I reckon the Owner has had a bellyful of social engagements.

We arrived before the dinner was quite over, to be parked at the end of the room at a long table laid out with extra menus and pamphlets setting down the scientific aims of the Expedition. I had a chance to glance at the menu and they'd had fillets of beef *Terra Nova*, soufflé *Captain Scott* and *South Pole* ice pudding.

It was a splendid dining-room, glittering with silver candelabras and gilded cornices, and you've never seen so many flowers, some in vases and others massed in

brass tubs, and all of them white – lilies, possibly – to go
with the theme of the white South, and a turkey carpet,
embroidered in blues and yellows, of such magnificence
that it seemed a crime to walk on it. There was a
continual buzz and drone of voices in one's ears, as if
bees had zoomed in on a garden heavy with blooms.

The Owner was seated dead-centre at the head table.
I could see him craning forward, trying to spot us, only
we were hidden, see, by a bloody big potted palm. Lt.
Bowers was there, and the Mate, and Mrs Evans, two
shoulders along from the Owner. I have to admit Mrs
Evans is a bit of a bobby-dazzler. She was dressed in
white, with a pale flower caught up in her dark hair.
Mrs Scott was seated to the left of the Lord Mayor. She
was sort of sprawled back in her chair looking bored,
and she was wearing purple.

There was no sign, of course, of Captain Oates. The
day before he'd told Lashly wild horses wouldn't drag
him to such a do, and that he was damned if he'd sit
down to dine with a bunch of Labour socialists. I'm not
convinced he's against such gatherings on political
grounds, any more than from shyness, rather that he's
so much his own man, and such a prey to boredom into
the bargain, that he does as he pleases.

Ten minutes or so after we'd sat down there was a lull
in the proceedings to allow the ladies to go to the
powder room, during which interlude the band
launched into a rendering of the *Hero of the South*. I
suspect Mrs Scott had kicked off her shoes, because she
was bent sideways searching for something under the
table, and when she finally rose to her feet she was a
little off balance, and the Owner took her by the elbow
to steady her. She smiled at him and flicked at his face,
playfully, with her napkin. You could tell by the way he

squeezed her arm they were friends, not just husband and wife.

One of the waiters wheeled a trolley at us with the remains of the South Pole pudding sliding sideways on a silver platter; Crean plucked the little flag off the top and stuck it behind his ear. 'If it's all the same to you,' I told the waiter, 'we'd prefer something stronger to cool our throats.'

A comic singer and a lady harpist were heralded as about to give of their all. The singer came on and sang a George Robey song about a philandering husband who took a girl to the music-hall and bumped into his wife, the chorus of which we all joined in with a will:

> Staring me in the face,
> Staring me in the face,
> There she was and that lodger of ours,
> Staring me in the face.

We could have done with more of him, but then the lady harpist scuttled in and you could tell from the general unrest and hubbub throughout that nobody was prepared to listen to that sort of tinkling. By way of amends for her less than enthusiastic reception she was given a tremendous ovation at the end, and the Lord Mayor presented her with a posy.

I had just settled down behind the palm fronds with a full glass in my hand when Mr Trevor Jones, Chairman of the Chamber, called upon the Lord Mayor to present the Owner with a flag emblazoned with the arms of the City of Cardiff. It was neatly folded when handed over, until the Owner, attempting to show suitable appreciation, made the mistake of opening it out. Yards of it fell across the tablecloth. Mrs Scott started to laugh. Then the Owner, struggling with its unwieldy folds, bellowed, 'Taff ... Taff Evans ... where are you?'

Clissold, the ship's cook, pushed me to my feet. He'd had a skinful by then and could have hurled me across the room by brute force. I would have dodged away, only the Owner, spying me, waved his arm and called, 'Taff, I need you.'

I bobbed up and down, feeling foolish, at which the Owner shouted out in ringing tones, 'My Lord Mayor, Ladies and Gentlemen, allow me to present my friend and fellow explorer, Petty Officer Evans.' Such an explosion of cheering and foot-stamping took place that it would have been the height of mock modesty not to show myself.

The Mate was relegated to the end of the Captain's table, so I could be placed between the Owner and the Lord Mayor. Mrs Scott was still laughing; I distinctly remember the Owner leaning across me and hissing, 'Kathleen, darling, for God's sake, do stop.' He got to his feet, thanked everyone for the flag – Lt. Bowers was all this time trying to confine it to manageable proportions – and promised it would be flying from the mast when we departed from Cardiff and hoisted again at the Pole. This last remark was a blatant lie. Where we're off to we're going to find it difficult enough to haul ourselves upright, never mind a flag that size.

'We shall never forget,' he said, 'the kindness of the City of Cardiff, where we have found the best coal, the best facilities, and the best backing any explorer could hope for.' Here he faltered, cleared his throat and was unable to continue. Most of those watching took it he was momentarily overcome with gratitude, but as Mrs Scott was still making strangled noises behind her napkin I reckoned he was struggling with an altogether different sort of emotion.

By now, Lt. Bowers had reduced the flag to the size of a folded tent and draped it over the back of his chair. Recovering, the Owner reached across and stroking it reverently, spoke the following words: 'I assure you we will never forget our welcome in Cardiff, or this flag. We would never have endured the strain of preparation except for the support of the people of South Wales. The memory of your generosity,' and here he spread out his arms to embrace the whole room, 'will inspire us in what I really believe is a great work.' Then he shifted the flag from the chair back and, turning to me, declared, 'I have no hesitation in entrusting this magnificent emblem into the safe-keeping of Petty Officer Edgar Evans, our 'Taff', a true son of Wales and the companion of my earlier voyage.'

I ask you, it would have gone to any man's head – all that cheering, the rapping on the tables for me to respond, the Owner smiling at me, the band striking up *Hen Wlad fy Nhadau*.

All things considered, I think I acquitted myself fairly well. I don't count myself as educated, but when I stood up I had a feeling in my head – and it was nothing to do with liquor – that I was part of something special, something with glory in it. Even before I opened my mouth a man with a white goatee beard shouted out, 'Nail our flag to the Pole, Taff Evans.' He wasn't joking. There was some laughter, though not as much as you'd expect, yet I didn't feel angry at such ignorance; if anything I was uplifted, see, at such simplicity, and there was this pride surging in my breast, pride that I was Welsh through and through.

For the Owner's benefit I translated into English the mottoes embroidered across the flag: *Awake the Day* and

The Welsh Dragon Leads the Van – at the time the words seemed profound, though in the cold light of day I can't see them as all that relevant.

'There is no one,' I said, 'save the Captain, who could have persuaded me to return to the South. He's the sort who inspires loyalty, respect ... love.' And here I dashed the moisture from my eye. I daresay the tears had a lot to do with the amount of drink I'd taken on board, but it isn't easy for a man to say what he feels unless he's in an exalted state, and I was expressing no more than the truth.

In a way I was glad my wife wasn't there to hear me, for though she would have been proud at my being king-pin she might also have considered she was taking second place in my affections. I noticed the Owner was looking very serious, properly moved this time he was, and Mrs Scott opened her reticule and took out her handkerchief, though in her case she was probably still in the grip of hilarity.

Then, to lighten the proceedings, I called out for the benefit of the fellow with the goatee: 'If we do reach the Pole, I hope to carry it home to Swansea rather than let it moulder in the National Museum of Cardiff.' Whereupon a stout alderman at another table offered me £10 if I'd chip off a piece and slip it to him privately. Quick as a flash I shouted back: 'Why not pay for it in advance?'

I ended my little speech with the words, 'We may die there ... and join poor Vince, clutched in the cold clasp of the ice ... but if we ever do come back, we hope to meet you in Cardiff.'

No sooner had I sat down than the stout man announced he was prepared to donate £500 to the fund. Someone else followed suit with an offer of £52 10s.

Within fifteen minutes cheques adding up to near a thousand pounds had been dumped on the Owner's pudding plate. 'Bless you, Taff,' the Owner said, shaking me vigorously by the hand, 'you're a bloody marvel', and I said, minding my manners, 'Pleased to be of assistance, sir. Sign off the Belgian stoker. He'll not last the course.'

Later I had a chat with the wife of the Lord Mayor. As soon as I heard myself claiming kinship with Lloyd George I made my excuses and legged it back to the ship. I didn't want to blot my copybook, not after such a triumphal night.

The following afternoon my niece Sarah arrived from Swansea to wish me godspeed. She's a clever girl and reads books out of the library. Right from a little one she's shown interest in my stories of the South, being particularly curious about the sort of birds you get out there, as well as fish. Once, she wrote a letter to Dr Wilson asking him some question or another, and with his reply he sent her a little sketch of snowy petrels. I've not seen it myself, but her mother says she's got it pinned up behind her bed with a bit of tissue-paper fixed on top to keep the dust off.

Sarah wanted to see over the *Terra Nova* right away. I was somewhat subdued after what Crean had told me at breakfast, and the last thing I wanted was her getting into conversation with any of the crew, not with events still fresh in their minds. It was a bit awkward; she could see for herself the ship was crawling with visitors. I had to pretend they were guests of the officers.

'You were in all the newspapers this morning, Uncle Edgar,' she said. 'You're more famous than any of the officers.'

'What's that supposed to mean?' I asked. 'What do they

say about me?'

'You raised a lot of money,' she said. 'By making a speech. They say you touched their hearts.'

'Did I indeed?' I said, feeling less alarmed, and promised that tomorrow I'd show her the scientific laboratory and the space where Dr Wilson would be doing his studying of birds, though I left out the fact they'd mostly be dead ones. She was stopping the night with my brother-in-law, so I gave her a few pence to buy herself a cup of tea and a cake and said I'd see her first thing in the morning.

There wasn't a peep out of Lt. Evans all day, not that I went out of my way to be in his vicinity. It's not that I'd be against urinating over his boots, particularly if he was looking in another direction at the time, but I'm inclined to think either some of the lads made the whole story up to agitate me, or else he was so far gone himself that he's none too sure of his own conduct. As for the flag, how it got draped over a tram at the terminus, beats me. If Jones the Goat hadn't spotted it, it could have travelled half way across Cardiff. Fortunately there's no harm done – Crean scrubbed off the stains at the pump and the sailmaker smoothed it out under the flat iron.

I didn't go ashore that last evening. There were a lot of jobs to see to, and besides, I thought it best to lie low. The Owner, poor devil, attended a buffet supper at the City Hall. I heard later it wasn't an occasion for speech-making, or conversation either for that matter, seeing Madame Hughes-Thomas's Royal Welsh Ladies' Choir sang throughout.

Lt. Bowers didn't go. He was up into the small hours making entries in his notebooks and stalking round his provision boxes like a broody hen. Nor was he in the mood for talk when I brought him his cocoa. I put his reserve down to anxiety; after all, none can know what may befall us. Thinking to put him at his ease, me being an old hand, I said it was a strange feeling, wasn't it, knowing that tomorrow we'd be gone.

'Strange?' he said. 'How so?'

'Why, after all this waiting, sir,' I said. 'It's like letting a dog off the leash and him none too sure where he wants to go any more.'

'I don't get your drift,' he said.

'It's a question of losing the scent, sir,' I said. 'Leastways, it strikes me as similar.'

'Not being a dog,' he replied, 'I'm afraid I have difficulty in following the allusion.'

'Yes, sir,' I said. 'Point taken, sir. I daresay our spirits will rise the moment we get up anchor.'

'Some of us,' he responded curtly, 'have never been low in spirits.'

From the stern look he flashed me I knew I was right about him being nervy. Who can blame him? The South is nothing like India.

I left him and went up on deck to look out at the slithering city, its glitter of street lamps fizzy under the rain. There's something wrong about a ship in dock, something pathetic, like a bird fluttering in a spill of oil. The *Nova* was tethered to her berth by ropes and chains, caught in a pool of greasy water. I could feel her shifting under my feet, tugging to be free. In spite of the late hour there were still groups of people come to stare up at her. I knew what they could see; a cat's-cradle of rigging illuminated by lanterns; a gleam of paint and brass work, the red burn of the cigar puffed on by the officer of the watch. The best of her was invisible, not to be described in words.

45

There are good ships and bad ships and the difference between them has nothing to do with being seaworthy. If I was fanciful I might say some had souls. There are ships built to withstand the worst the Almighty can throw at them yet they go down with hardly a murmur, and there are other, frailer craft, who, having battled the winds and lost masts, yards and canvas, still bob safe home to harbour. With experience a man can tell the one from the other the moment he steps aboard, neither from look nor feel, but from something fathoms deep within himself.

I stayed on deck for over an hour, hoping to have a quiet last word with the owner, until I remembered he was a guest at the Mansion House.

*

The Belgian left just before midday. I ran into him between decks when I was showing Sarah over the ship. He didn't say anything, nor did I, and I pretended not to notice he had his kit-bag slung over his shoulder. We nodded as we passed and that was that.

Some minutes later the Chief Steward said the Owner wanted to see me in his cabin. I took my niece with me, as a precaution. I reckoned if he had heard any gossip about that business of the flag he was hardly likely to haul me over the coals in the present of a third party, and a relation at that. It turned out the Lord Mayor wanted to say goodbye to me personally and present me with a photograph of himself. He'd already given me one, at the smoking concert, which means his recollection of the occasion is as hazy as mine. I hadn't set eyes on the first photograph since one of his flunkeys handed it to me before I spun out through the

revolving doors of the Royal Hotel. I daresay, the
Mayor being no oil painting, it's going backwards and
forwards on some tram in the city.

Mrs Scott was there too, and Dr Wilson. The doctor
put himself out to be pleasant to Sarah. She asked him if
there were any books to do with birds that he would
particularly recommend she should read. There and
then he made her out a list. While he was talking to her I
overheard the Lord Mayor say something to the Owner
about the 'hazardous task' ahead, and whether he
thought it would be accomplished. The Owner replied,
'I will reach the South Pole, or I will never come back
again', at which Mrs Scott exclaimed, 'Con, my dearest,
you will succeed.'

We moved away from the dockside at one o'clock, the
tug *Falcon* attached to our bow and the *Bantam Cock* to the
stern. You've never heard such a coronation roar as went
up when we were towed through the lock-gates; hooters
and sirens whooping like devils, bands playing, deto-
nators and guns firing, thousands of people hurrahing
under the drizzling rain. Even when we got out into the
Channel we were still surrounded by pleasure boats, their
rails lined six deep with cheering passengers. We'd
hauled aloft the Cardiff flag at the fore and the Welsh flag
at the mizen, and one of the officers – Captain Oates, I
expect – had hung two large leeks up with the latter, and
some wag belonging to the Chamber of Commerce bellowed through the hailer that he hoped we'd left the
Welsh 'leak' behind. We hadn't; indeed, when the tugs let
go and we began to sail under our own steam it became
only too apparent we'd gained a few more.

In the late afternoon, off the Breaksea Lightship, the
Owner and the Lord Mayor's party quitted the *Terra
Nova*. He had the crew assembled aft to shake hands with

him; he didn't have a special word for me, simply looked me in the eye and passed on down the line. Then he said, 'It has taken a long time and you have served me well. We are all contributing to a great enterprise which is only just beginning. Each and every one of you will play your part. I wish you godspeed and look forward to joining you at Simonstown.'

It was still raining and a light breeze had sprung up. Mrs Scott held on to her hat as she was helped aboard the tug. Those of the after-guard not at the pumps stayed at the rail to cheer the Owner away. I doubt if he heard us; the military band aboard the *Falcon* was playing *Auld Lang Syne*, the tune coming in rags across the darkening water.

Dr Edward (Uncle Bill) Wilson
July 1910

We spent three days at Madeira, taking on supplies, during which time I took the opportunity to make an excursion to the Palheiro with Titus Oates and Birdie Bowers. We rode upwards among Portuguese laurels and camellia trees growing forty-foot high. After a quarter of an hour Titus said he couldn't stand the slow pace; pressing his heels to the sides of his mule as though he was out hunting, he wheeled about and slithered back down the winding path in a flurry of dust.

The scenery was magnificent; abrupt precipices, wooded hills and crags, tumbling waters and a paradise of mosses, ferns and pink belladonna lilies. One moment the air was polluted with the odour of the black til (Oreodaphne foetens), so named because of its awful smell, and the next filled with the delicious scent of the beautiful lily of the valley tree (Clethra arborea).

Halfway up we overtook a procession of mourners carrying a dead child in a litter. We dismounted, out of respect, and had a good view of the small corpse draped in white lace, its doll-like hands clasped on its breast. There was another child, whose duty it was to keep the flies away. He was smugly smiling, proud of his responsibility, dashing a palm frond to and fro above the bier.

From the Palheiro we rode across to the Curral dos Romeiros to look at the Mount Church associated with so many miracles. Birdie was particularly taken with the one concerning the Virgin. The island being caught in the grip of famine, the inhabitants climbed in procession to the church and prayed to the statue of the Madonna for deliverance. Next day a ship loaded with grain came into the harbour, and the statue of the Madonna was found to be dripping with moisture. Some even claimed to have seen the Virgin swimming ahead of the ship, towing her in with the cable between her teeth!

Not far from the church is Monte Quinta, with a splendid view from its summit of the Bay of Funchal and the blue ocean beyond. Birdie's enthusiasm was touching; he is a fellow after my own heart, being possessed of many enviable qualities – self-abnegation, curiosity, a capacity for hard work, meticulous attention to detail, and above all, an unsung yet deep-rooted belief in the love of God.

His face glowed brick-red, and he perspired so freely I feared he might melt before my eyes. He said he hated the heat and heartily took issue with Dante in placing the circle of ice below that of fire as the worst of all torments.

I told him he might have cause to change his mind once we reached our destination.

'I very much doubt it,' he replied. 'Excessive heat brings raging thirst, fever and delirium, whereas the cold, from what I've read, merely numbs the mind and positively lulls one into sleep.'

He's possibly in the right of it. Though I have only to glance at the scars on my hand to remind myself of the damaging effects of low temperatures, I would have to read the notes I made at the time to recall the true horror of that first expedition. The experience, once a blazing nightmare, has long since faded to a chilly dream.

That being said, any doubts I may have had about the wisdom of coming south again have evaporated like snow under sunlight. After five weeks at sea I'm as fit as a fiddle and have actually put on weight. It's a blessed thing to be driven by hard work, because one never feels the want of exercise. I may spend a good deal of my time standing stationary, endeavouring to turn out water-colours of the sea and the sky; but trying to keep balanced against the roll of the ship requires the use of muscles I scarcely knew existed outside the pages of an anatomy book. There is also nothing more fatiguing and laborious than a four-hour stint at the pumps. As for transferring coal from the main hold to the bunkers – within ten minutes I'm streaming with sweat and as black as a Kaffir.

I cannot imagine now why the thought of leaving my work and committing myself to three years away from home caused me so much anguish. I tremble sometimes to think of what a wrench it was to leave my dear wife Oriana, and how quickly I have adapted to the parting. I can only suppose that it's in a man's nature, and mine in particular, to bury regrets and make the best of things once a decision has been made.

I'm fortunate, of course, in that my fellow voyagers have turned out to be so congenial. With the exception of one or two, and I readily admit my antipathy towards them springs not so much from their defects as from my own deplorable lack of tolerance, one couldn't wish for more delightful companions. Campbell will make an excellent leader, Pennell and Atkinson are absolutely splendid, Nelson a perfect treasure, and young Cherry Garrard as deserving of encouragement as any man I've met. As for Titus Oates, I'm beginning to suspect there is a great deal more to him than his air of amused taciturnity would have us believe.

And then there's Birdie: it strikes me as mysterious the way the right man emerges just when destiny has need of him. I really believe Bowers to have been placed at our disposal by something other than chance. Listening to his history – and he's the most modest of fellows – his navigation of the *Irrawady*, his accounts of shore-leaves spent bicycling across India, through terrain menaced by bear, leopard and elephant with nothing more formidable than a butterfly net strapped to his back, one can only marvel at his endurance.

Con recognised his worth at once, which is why he signed him on. The rest of us took him at face value; we thought him too young, too unprepossessing, too short of stature to rise above the common herd. We should have remembered Napoleon.

Just before dinner the other evening Nelson spotted a Portuguese man-of-war floating in its glassy bubble off the port side. They're astonishingly beautiful in their natural element, reflecting water and sky. Once removed from the sea they go out like a candle, the colour snuffed away. I did a painting of it, all the same. Birdie, studying both the finished water-colour and the shrunken original, remarked how obviously the finger of God illuminates the animate world.

It's significant, after so short a time, how we have all shaken down and begun to work as a team. Birdie and I are usually the first up in the morning. The ship now having run into the doldrums, and below decks often as steamy as a Turkish bath, we sleep on top of the ice-house. There are few more enjoyable experiences in this world than lying under the shooting stars to the sound of the wind moaning through the rigging, and the voice of dear old Birdie asking his interminable questions.

First job for everyone is a stint at the pumps – the ancient ship leaks like a sieve – after which some of us go over the side to bathe and others make do with hauling up buckets of sea water. I must say I'm considerably less enamoured of the former method since a shark made a beeline for Birdie. He, not at all put out, merely removed that absurd green hat he wears at all times and sweeping it round above his head hollered so loudly the shark took fright and fled. When I asked him if he had not felt afraid, he said, 'Certainly, Uncle Bill, but it wouldn't have done to let the beggar know it.'

When it rains, as it frequently does in these latitudes, you've never seen such a sight topside. The entire ship's company strips off and stands naked beneath the tropical downpour. Some of us take the opportunity to wash our clothes in the stream that forms between the laboratories and the ward-room skylight.

By eight o'clock I'm generally in the crow's-nest with my sketch-book and colours. The sunsets and sunrises in these regions are spectacular. Sometimes the equatorial sky resembles a vast continent soaring above us, its snow-capped mountains ringed with fire, its blue oceans edged by shores of blazing gold. At others, the clouds, sliding from pink to green to sullen purple, press so low that the ship quivers and stands still, stuck in black water under the bell-jar of the heavens, until, as though some mighty artery had burst, the sun nudges the horizon and stains the world with crimson light.

For two or three hours I make my poor attempts to capture such wonderful effects on paper, and then continue my work on Lord Lovat's survey of diseases in grouse which I hope to complete by the time we reach Simonstown. Any odd hour left over sees me at the ward-room table working out sledging rations for the depot journey.

Lord knows what I should do if the crow's-nest wasn't available to me. Quite apart from its being the best vantage point from which to work, it also enables me to be solitary. Constant companionship exhausts me, and but for my lonely hours up against the sky I would find the boisterous evenings unbearable. I'm something of a dull fish, and though I'm flattered when one or other of the chaps come to me with their grievances – and sooner or later they all do – I'm much afraid that my reputation for patience and impartiality stems more from lassitude than involvement. Better to say nothing than to condemn, and to laugh with than to criticise, and so *much* happier.

Con is far more intuitive than I am. For example: upon first meeting Cherry-Garrard he deduced him to be a timid young man, much diminished by a domineering father and an over-protective mother. I haven't the slightest idea how he reached such a conclusion on such short acquaintance, but I daresay he's right. I have no quarrel with his additional observation that Cherry's heart is in the right place.

The fact that we all mix so well is greatly to the credit of Teddy Evans. Though he could be considered somewhat lightweight, a little too boyish at all times, his lack of complexity and absence of moods are in the best interests of those under his command. The men respond to him well, and he seems to bear not the smallest grudge towards Petty Officer Evans, whose drunken behaviour after the Lord Mayor's reception in Cardiff – it took six men to carry him back to the ship – caused so much personal affront. What one needs in these cramped conditions is to be under the government of a sunny disposition, and in this respect Teddy more than fills the bill.

He's the leader of the pack when it comes to ragging; it was he who instigated the originally innocent game of 'The Parish Priest Has Lost His Cap', which now ends with the entire ward-room losing their trousers. I haven't laughed so much in years. Titus says he's never known a rowdier mess, yet it's all good clean fun. We behave as though we were June boys again, waiting to go into bat, and I'm convinced that these frequent displays of bubbling high spirits bode well for the greater game ahead.

Last night, lying alongside each other in our sleeping-bags on top of the ice-house, and having exhausted me with his queries as to the reproductive processes of dolphins, thrashers and kingfish, Birdie asked me what I thought of Con. 'You're close to him, Bill,' he said. 'I have enormous respect for him myself, but I'd value your opinion.'

'He's the best,' I replied, without hesitation. 'If he seems unapproachable at times, it's to do with his sense of fair play. He doesn't want to appear to have favourites. He once confided that although he considers the sea his whole life and wouldn't have it otherwise he nevertheless feels something of a misfit.'

Birdie immediately wanted to know what I meant. I tried to explain how Con has often thought that being subjected to Naval discipline at such an early age, hardly more than a child, has perhaps turned him from what might have been his true direction. 'He fancies it has made him too rigid in his ways, too protective of himself.'

'When I was a boy on the *Worcester*,' Birdie said, 'they dragged me under the hose every morning and scrubbed me with a deck brush until I bled. Particularly my nose, it being so prominent.'

'You poor old fellow,' I exclaimed, and meant it. He must have been such a very small boy.

'What direction might he have gone in?' he suddenly enquired.

'I'm not sure,' I told him. 'And nor is he, his nature being a peculiar mixture of the man of action and the dreamer ...' And here I trailed into silence, feeling I had already said far too much, at which Birdie, sensitive fellow that he is, changed tack instantly and chirruped that he couldn't wait to see South Trinidad Island.

Thinking about my wife in the warm darkness it occurred to me there is something of the female in both Con and Birdie, though it surfaces in different ways: while only one is capricious, both are equally perceptive.

I'm not altogether sure Oriana cares for Con, any more than she admires Kathleen Scott. I'm in favour of Mrs S, even if she is a little too forthright in her ways and not at all inclined to take a back seat, for there's no denying she's made Scott a happier man. She once informed me, without the trace of a smile, that she couldn't stand women and would much prefer the world to be composed entirely of men and children.

It's understandable, I suppose, that Oriana should regard Con as something of a rival, he being the one to entice me from her side. When we discussed whether I should go south I told her I felt Con needed me, that in many ways I regarded him as my responsibility.

'And then, of course,' she said, 'you have such a feeling of the absolute necessity to be doing something, at any hour of the day or night ... before the end comes.'

I have often found that women reach the heart of the matter without having the faintest idea of the route.

*

Something happened to me on the morning of July 16th – the ninth anniversary of my wedding-day – which disturbs me. It was dawn, and I was standing in the crow's-nest trying to see what effects might be achieved by dragging my thumb across a wash of vermilion water-colour, humming a Schubert song, the one Oriana sang the night we first met, when suddenly my head was filled with pictures of my time at medical school.

In those days, and I cringe now to think what a prig I was, I seriously considered becoming a missionary. My father was very much against it, as well he might be. He had supported me, without complaint, through three years of university and two years of medical training at St George's Hospital, and here I was about to throw it all up in favour of Africa. He didn't tell me it was out of the question; he simply suggested I should defer a decision until I had passed my final exams.

The conceit that I might be cut out to help others doubtless stemmed from my experiences as a Sunday School teacher at the Caius Mission in Battersea, where I read Bible stories to the children and gave lantern-slide lectures on life in other lands. I have never forgotten that slum brat who attended with eyes bandaged, both being bunged up with ophthalmia and blepharitis. At each change of the slide he would peer up from his grimy bandages for a second or so, and then hide his head in his hands until he heard the click of the lantern heralding the next.

It was hardly a bed of roses teaching those unwashed children – the girls smelled worse than the boys, for some brought babies with them, who howled throughout, and what with their wailing and the cry of the Hokey-Pokey man in the street outside, not to mention the Church Army band practising in the hall next door, I sometimes went home with my voice a mere croak.

I was seeing the mission-room in my mind's eye, those rows of shaven heads illuminated in a slant of sunlight writhing with dust, when, by some trick of the early light in the sky above me, the sea below broke into a thousand glittering fragments, and in that heavenly dazzle I clearly saw a creature, half man, half bird, soaring above the waves.

A moment before I had been as warm as toast, and now I was so cold I shuddered, and in that shuddering blinked, and the creature was gone, though not before I had gazed down into those lidless eyes fixed on mine, observed where its powerful shoulders jutted into wings, followed the silver spray kicked up by its cruel talons as it skimmed the bright water. There was no doubt in my mind that the apparition was a harbinger of death and yet, in the blaze of that terrible second a sensation akin to joy, something pitched between sexual arousal and fear bubbled up inside me. Still my body shook, and through chattering teeth I heard myself stuttering over and over, 'So cold ... so cold ... so cold.'

I don't know how long the trembling lasted; time itself stood still. It was but gradually that I became aware of my surroundings: the sea, dark blue and choppy, the sun continuing to flood the horizon, my hand with its bloodied thumb quivering on the surface of my sketching-pad.

I have thought of an explanation, though it's far from rational. In my first year as a Junior House Surgeon one of my fingers became infected after conducting a post-mortem, and I was reduced to slicing the swollen skin to bleed out the poison. This, and the recollection of that boy with the bandaged eyes, had led perhaps to a juxtaposition of the natural and the spiritual world, lifted that inner shutter on the mind which generally confines us in the dark and blinds us to things undreamt of in our philosophy.

That I was alarmed by this omen – portent, call it what you will – puzzles me, because I'm no stranger to death. Indeed, there was a period after I'd contracted tuberculosis when I ran to greet it. My life, then, revolved round bacilli and expectoration and the precise amount of perspiration lost in the feverish nights, and I was weary of it. Worst of all was my having to do without tobacco. For some months I persisted in smoking, but finally the bouts of coughing that followed each blissful inhalation outweighed the pleasure. There was an afternoon in the Alps – I had climbed 8000 feet above the Dischma valley, the pleuritic pains in my lungs echoed in my ribs and back, my wretched pulse pounding at the rate of 168 per minute – when I almost gave up the fight and would willingly have left this world. Wanting to die isn't a sin, merely the presumption that one can choose the moment. I crouched on a clump of grass, clutching a bunch of saxifrage in flower to my heaving chest, and waited: not so much for the end as a beginning. Then, from somewhere below, beyond the green larches and the purple meadows, I heard a Great Spotted Woodpecker rattling in a fir wood, and I caught my breath and knew I must stay, if only to fulfil the purpose – whatever that may be – for which I've been put on this earth.

God moves in mysterious ways. A year later, having applied for the post of junior surgeon and zoologist to the Polar Expedition of 1901, I sailed south. Where sunshine, wholesome food and mountain air had failed to heal my diseased lungs, hunger, frost-bite and ordeal by blizzard affected a cure. As the body lives so does the the spirit, and both must be born, and broken, in order to reach the light.

I didn't tell anyone about that glittering bird for several days. Then, just past midnight on the 23rd a fearful racket broke out on deck and I woke on the ice-house to find Rennick, Teddy Evans and Birdie dancing and singing by starlight on top of the main hatch dog-kennel. This impromptu war dance turned out to be in celebration of my thirty-eighth birthday and succeeded in rousing everyone on board.

Later, we had a tremendous scrap in which Cherry, Campbell and I held the Nursery against the rest of the ward-room. The Nursery, originally designed to accommodate four, and now sleeping six of the younger members of the scientific staff as well as housing the pianola, forms the gangway between the engine room and the ward-room. There is only one door, and such was the crush, not to mention the combined charges of Oates and Atkinson as they hurled themselves against the wood, it's a miracle it withstood the onslaught and remained in one piece. Likewise ourselves; half of us were naked at the finish, having had the clothes torn off our backs. I can't think this sort of behaviour will continue once Con takes command. He's not a spoil-sport by any means, but I reckon his presence will put a damper on our exuberance.

It wasn't until the small hours that I climbed back into my sleeping bag and, turning to Birdie, confided what I had seen that dawn morning the previous week. I knew for certain he would listen sympathetically. Otherwise I wouldn't have opened my mouth, though I daresay my tongue was somewhat loosened by the quantities of wine I'd downed. Nor did I imagine he'd be so foolish as to suggest I'd seen an extra large albatross – all the same, I was unprepared for his response.

'I expect,' I told him, having described the dazzling light between water and sky, 'that it was some trick of the rising sun, some mirage conjured up by the inner eye.'

'I don't agree, Uncle Bill,' he said. 'It's true that some of us see what we want to see, but I don't put you in that category. That apart, I know from first-hand experience there are some things we should accept for what they are.' And then he told me the following story:

'I was serving as third mate on the *Loch Torridon* in the spring of 1902. I wasn't very happy ... due to circum-stances I won't go into. It wasn't a contented ship; the captain was no good and every time we put into port one or other of the crew deserted. We berthed at Adelaide to take on sulphide ore, tallow and wheat. The steward jumped ship and I had to go into town to get the cook out of jail. The new crew came on board fighting drunk. There was one chap in particular, a brute with a golden eagle tattooed on his bald pate, who would make Petty Officer Evans look like an angel.'

'Come now,' I interrupted, 'be fair. Evans is an excellent worker and he hasn't touched a drop since we left Cardiff.'

'Point taken,' Birdie said. 'At any rate, this fellow was a swine and he made my life a misery. I tried to persuade the Captain to dismiss him but he wouldn't hear of it. Eventually, at three o'clock in the morning we got up anchor, trimmed yards, set sails and were off. I was at my lowest. I'd been reading a lot, you see, thinking about things ... all sorts of things. I was bothered about leaving my mother. She doesn't really like the career I've chosen, and yet she's never stopped me. I'm her only son. It's made me feel selfish, taken the joy out of it.'

He peered at me in the darkness to see if I understood. I didn't, not altogether. It's a thing Con and he and Cherry and Titus Oates all share, this bond with their mothers – but then, of course, their fathers are long since dead, whereas mine is alive. It was dear old Dad who fostered my interest in botany and encouraged me to go on walking tours through the countryside, so it's only natural I should feel closer to him than to my mother, there being so much more we have in common. When I was at Cambridge my mother wrote complaining I never allowed her to know what I really thought, that I was too reserved. I tore her letter into bits, but the sentences remain intact in my head.

'I expect I was lonely,' Birdie said. 'Life at sea makes one so dependent on nature.'

'I can't see you suffering from loneliness,' I protested. 'Anyone but you.'

'Not *suffering*,' Birdie objected. 'Just that from time to time one has a need to share one's disappointments with someone ... someone special.'

It occurred to me he was talking about women. He has mentioned, more than once, some girls he met in Melbourne, sisters who entertained him and his

fellow-officers one weekend and who later sent him a
pot of home-made jam, but it's unthinkable to imagine
he's anything but utterly virginal in both mind and
body. In Madeira, at the various functions we were
required to attend, he was the life and soul of the party,
yet when he was obliged to get up and dance he turned
scarlet. There was something irresistibly comical about
his appearance as he capered boisterously and
hopelessly out of step about the polished floor. Some
men look right against any background, Con among
them. Not Birdie; away from the sea and out of uniform
he could be mistaken for a diminutive rent-collector.
See him on deck though, muscular legs braced against
the roll of the ship, and he comes into his element. He
keeps the empty jamjar in his locker.

'That night,' Birdie continued, 'I swear Christ came to
me ... not in any recognisable shape, that is ... no haloes
or long nightshirts, or anything of that sort ... all the
same, He was there ...'

'But my dear Birdie,' I protested, 'there was nothing
of Christ in the creature I saw. On the contrary, it had
more in common with the devil.'

'You can't have one without the other,' he argued.
'Ever since that night I fancy I know what's important. I
also know that my overriding ambition to get on in the
world conflicts with my spiritual growth.'

'I'm ambitious too,' I blurted out, and surprised
myself; it's not something I'm proud of. I remember
taking my drawings to some gallery in London and their
being rejected. I'd expected they would be, yet I never
dreamt I would feel so angry. Con's ambitious too, but
he's more honest about it, or rather the doubting
Thomas part of his character enables him to put things
in perspective. I walk backwards, though deep down I

imagine I'm worthy enough to be in the forefront. Con strides ahead and doesn't really believe leadership is worth a toss.

It often strikes me that Con and myself, Birdie and Oates, even Peter Pan Evans with his penchant for swinging one round by the seat of the trousers, are the misfits, victims of a changing world. It's difficult for a man to know where he fits in any more. All the things we were taught to believe in, love of country, of Empire, of devotion to duty, are being held up to ridicule. The validity of the class system, the motives of respectable, educated men are now as much under the scrutiny of the magnifying glass as the parasites feeding off the Scottish grouse. Such a dissection of purpose is unsettling and has possibly led me to hide my ambition behind a shield of puritanism. How significant it is that the words 'naked' and 'ambition' are so often linked.

'It seems to me,' Birdie said, 'that we have to make a choice between the spiritual and the material world, and if we can't become saints then we must find a sort of balance which will allow us to be at peace with ourselves. All I know is, nothing matters a damn except that we should help one another.'

I was enormously impressed at his ability to put such thoughts into words. I may think as he does, but it's beyond me to express myself so naturally; I'm far too wary of being taken for an ass.

'Listen,' he said. 'I'm awfully afraid I won't be up to it when we reach the South. You'll have to be prepared for me to lean on you.'

I laughed, for the idea of Birdie turning to anyone for help struck me as absurd. 'My dear boy, you're the best equipped of any of us. If I could get through it while still an invalid, I'm quite sure you'll romp home with flying colours.'

He didn't answer, and I thought he was lost in contemplation. A moment later he snored so loudly it woke him up and I heard him mutter, 'It's good to know the cold won't rot us.'

In spite of our little chat I still feel uneasy. It's hard to wipe from my mind the memory of those lidless, malevolent eyes.

*

We sighted South Trinidad Island two days later, furled sail and lay four miles off. Birdie agreed I hadn't exaggerated its sinister appearance. Then night fell and moonlight transformed it into a fairy castle, towers, turrets and battlements touched with silver. Birdie stayed awake half the night, rhapsodising on its beauty and wishing his mother was there to see it. Every time a bird wheeled overhead he nudged me in the ribs demanding to know if it was *my* bird. I'd been vain enough to tell him that when we stopped here in 1901 Con had insisted on calling a previously unknown species of petrel after me. It's rot, of course, but nice all the same to know a bird exists bearing the name Aestrelata Wilsoni. The fact that it makes a noise somewhere between the demented hoot of a cuckoo and the drumming of a snipe is neither here nor there.

At half past five in the morning when we steamed closer, the reality of the island was more daunting. The mountains of volcanic rock twisted into jagged shapes, slashed by ravines and violently veined with basaltic deposits coloured mustard yellow and metallic red, the cascades of purple and black debris, rose sheer from the boiling surf. Though the day was clear, without cloud, a veil of dense vapour curled about the summit, through which the inky pinnacles thrust upwards to meet the rosy dawn.

A forest of dead trees covers the island, interspersed with ferns which grow to a height of eighteen feet and a species of acacia and flowering bean. What little soil there is consists of a loose powder, almost like volcanic ash. The few sandy beaches, split by landslips of coal-black rock tumbling a thousand feet, are strewn with wreckage and alive with sea crabs.

The most reasonable explanation for the decayed trees would seem to be that at some time, and not so far distant as one might suppose, an eruption of lava took place which consumed everything in its path. Either that or the place was engulfed in a tidal wave of such proportions that its vegetation was utterly destroyed by salt water. I have heard that in the seventeen hundreds the island was a penal settlement. There are written accounts of the ruins of primitive huts being found on the weather side. One can only shudder at the thought of being consigned for life to such a God-forsaken place.

Cautiously, such was the menacing roar of the breakers as they dashed against the cliffs, we coasted under the lee of the island and arriving at West Bay let go the anchor in fifteen fathoms. Teddy Evans had been all for continuing to South West Bay. The Admiralty chart lists it as clean with a uniform depth of ten fathoms, but I happen to know from my previous visit that it's full of sunken rocks. More important, it's entirely exposed to the storm wind of these seas, the dreaded *pampero*.

I also knew, from various documents lodged with the Royal Geographical Society, of the apparent foolhardiness of attempting a landing in June, July or August, these being the winter months in this latitude.

All the same, I kept quiet. Apart from manning the pumps morning, noon and night, we've had an easy passage. We needed some kind of physical adventure to tone us up for the privations ahead. In such situations I go against my natural caution and attempt to think like Con.

To my relief the water in West Bay was as smooth as a millpond, so much so that we could see the anchor below and the swarm of fish – shark, dolphin and rock-cod – which instantly flickered about its cable. We got out the whaler and the pram, and stowing the latter with guns, knives, rum, ship's biscuit, tobacco and fresh water, rowed off. It took some time to find a secure landing; then, coming across a natural pier formed of fallen rock, and more by good luck than judgment, we managed to scramble ashore.

The entomological party, comprised of Wright, Birdie and Teddy Evans, prepared to tramp inland. I felt alarmed for Birdie for he has a horror of insects, and spiders in particular. In Rangoon, when very young, while his mother was bathing him in preparation for bed, a tarantula climbed up the wall beside the tub. Upon his mother calling for help the houseboy ran in and squashed it with a slipper, at which it slid in a smear of burst slime, legs still obscenely twitching, and plopped into the water to float above the child's knee.

Knowing of this incident I suggested to Birdie that he accompany Cherry and myself. He wouldn't hear of it. 'Good of you, Uncle Bill' was what he said, 'but it's absolutely no good to run away from things.'

Oates, in partnership with Atkinson, who besides being a competent surgeon is an authority on bacteria, decided to make for the Cape below the Ninepin, leaving Cherry-Garrard and myself to climb southwards in the direction of the Sugarloaf on the weather side of the island, both parties in search of birds to shoot and eggs to collect.

We had with us Seaman Murphy, a garrulous character from Liverpool, whom I'd been treating for stomach cramps, and who I'd thought would benefit from a day in the fresh air. For all I know he was malingering, but I wasn't taking any chances because he'd only come aboard at the last minute in Cardiff as a replacement for a Belgian Con had suddenly taken against and dismissed.

It had been the intention that my patient would loaf about on the beach; I'd forgotten those loathsome, goggle-eyed, yellow-shelled land-crabs which crawl in their thousands about the island. Confront them, throw any kind of edible mess in their path, and they stand there staring you in the face with an almost diabolical expression, pulling the food to pieces in their front claws before bringing the fragments to their mouths and commencing to chew. They don't slabber, and I daresay, not having eyelids, they can't help looking devilish, but they do bear an uncanny resemblance to diners at some fish restaurant in the Strand. Lapse into a doze, daydream under the warm rain and they scuttle up to nip your neck and nibble your boots. Though I don't imagine they could kill a healthy man, I didn't like leaving an incapacitated one at their mercy.

Murphy, however, insisted he was more than able to look after himself. 'Don't you fret, sir,' he said. 'I'll let the buggers have it, sir, and no mistake, if they come within a mile of my bunions.' We settled him under a makeshift awning, the supplies heaped about him, and took the precaution of hiding the rum ration where he couldn't find it.

The setting off of the shooting parties was the cause of much merriment, the Trinidad petrel being so unused to humans as to regard us as nothing more threatening than so many ledges on which to perch, Birdie's green hat attracting particular attention. Oates, grimacing in disgust and wielding his weapon like a stick, said we might as well leave the lead shot behind as the barrels of our guns would be equally effective.

It took Cherry and me a laborious three hours to work our way towards the Sugarloaf. The ground is so rotten that often it was like walking a treadmill – no sooner had we managed to clamber a few feet than the surface crumbled away beneath us and we slid backwards again. With each resulting landslide the colonies of gannets and boobies perched on the surrounding rocks rose in a frenzy of beating wings and swooped about our heads. It was child's play picking up the eggs which are deposited like stones and without benefit of nests in every available hollow.

Backs aching, we crossed the Sugarloaf Col, slid down to the coast of South-East Bay and plodded along a shore marked with the tracks of turtles. At last, and I welcomed it, Cherry suggested we'd earned a rest. I'd given my ankle a severe knock when landing, and it was a relief to loosen my boot and rub the bruised bone.

The bay was littered with the wreckage of ships; planks, hencoops, barrels, empty gin bottles, and the picked haunches of a pig. Cherry remarked, in his good-hearted, sentimental way, that the skeleton of man or beast was a rude reminder of the fragility of the body. I knew what he was thinking; it's an exceptional man who doesn't at some time or other glimpse death in every fallen leaf. By way of response I let my face fall into a thoughtful mask. In my head I was remembering the last time I ate roast pork – on land, that is – that last Sunday when we stopped off at Oriana's parents for lunch before travelling on to Cardiff.

Oriana wasn't feeling too well. She'd had to lie down before the meal was finished, and on my going upstairs to see how she was she turned her head away when I bent to kiss her cheek; she said I had grease on my chin. I suspect she was upset I had shown such a hearty appetite for food when we were so soon to be parted.

Cherry kicked sand over those bleached bones and when everything was covered tramped up and down to smooth the surface. I half expected him to fashion a make-shift cross from driftwood to stick on the mound. He's very young. He'd taken off his glasses to clean them on his shirt and though his face was burnt by the sun his anxious eyes were ringed with white moons. 'Spectacles are an awful nuisance,' he complained, peering short-sightedly about him. 'The slightest exertion and they mist over. Either that or the sweat makes them slide down one's nose.'

'You may find them something of a handicap in the cold,' I warned him. 'They're bound to freeze over.'

'I expect I shall manage,' he said. 'Poor sight is something I've learnt to live with.'

I turned my face away from the sea. There was a stiff breeze blowing and I swear I could smell, mixed with the faintest trace of cooling, mushed apple, the aroma of pork crackling basted in hot honey.

'Uncle Bill,' asked Cherry suddenly, still kicking at the sand in that boyish way. 'Is it true that adversity brings out the best in men?'

'Yes,' I replied promptly. 'Good men, that is', and looked him straight in the eye, knowing he was thinking of the journey ahead and whether he was up to it, and wanting to tell him, without using words, that in my book he was.

'Men from our background,' I explained, 'are at an advantage. They've been schooled to accept things, not to argue the toss once the umpire has made a decision. Abiding by the rules is a great help, you know ... it does away with introspection, leaves one free to get on with the game.'

'I was never very much good at sport,' Cherry said, 'on account of my eyesight ... apart from rowing, that is, though even there I failed to get a blue. I'm afraid I was a disappointment to my father', and he smiled at me apologetically, as if I was someone else he'd let down.

I shirked taking him up on this, having been told about his father by Con, who maintains that the reason Cherry didn't do well at Oxford was because his old man treated him like a skivvy during the vacations.

'I can't tell you,' I said, 'what hell Royds went through in 1901 trying to pit his will against Scott's. He simply couldn't accept authority, any more than could Shackleton.'

I didn't think it fit to say more. I'd remembered the morning Shackleton accidentally burned a hole in the tent floor while cooking, and the broadside Con gave him. It had happened many times before, this spilling of oil and the subsequent blaze. We'd all done it, including Con. It's hard to behave like a Boy Scout boiling a billycan on the village green when the cold has paralysed one's mind and swollen one's fingers to the size of bananas. Taff Evans hadn't got a wigging. On the contrary, Con had told him not to worry and that he was sure we were all grateful for the warmth, however unexpected – but then Con has always had an exaggerated regard for the lower classes.

Some two days after Shackleton had set alight to the ground sheet he and I were employed in packing sledges. I daresay we were making a fair amount of noise, he laughing and me protesting at an indelicate story he'd just spun concerning a Grenadier Guard and an amorous batman. In those days, having been married for less than two months, I was far more prudish than I am now and I seem to remember I was trying to stuff his head into one of the sleeping bags. Just then Con came out of his tent and shouted, 'Come here, you bloody fools', only he used a stronger word.

Going up to him I said, 'I trust you weren't speaking to me, Con?' and he said, 'No, I wasn't, Bill.'

'In that case,' Shackeleton challenged, 'you meant me', at which Con stared him out. 'Right,' said Shackleton, standing his ground like a bantam cock, 'perhaps you should bear this in mind. You're the worst ——— fool of the lot, with ——— bells on.'

It wasn't until some years later I realised Con was upset at me for being so pally with Shackleton. He'd taken it on board that I was *his man*. That and the fact that earlier, while trying to get the dogs into the traces, he'd been bitten by one of the bitches.

With Con it's all or nothing, which is in part why I admire him. It sounds blasphemous, but one only has the energy to die for one man at a time.

'Is it nothing more than a game?' asked Cherry, wistfully, staring at me owl-eyed. Re-tying the laces of my boot, I stood up and busied myself with the fastenings of my back-pack. I didn't consider it advisable to continue the discussion; one can never be sure where such conversations may lead.

We followed the shore line until we came to East Bay, where the sheer wall of Noah's Ark mountain, rust red in the sunlight, dropped into the angry surf. There wasn't a beach as such, merely a tumbled floor of shattered rocks over which lay solidified streams of black lava. I'm constrained to think, from the quantity of debris and the tempestuous shapes which mimic the surge of waves, that the mountain was once an active volcano.

We proceeded on our way until we came to the magnificent tunnel known as the Archway which connects South West Bay with East Bay. The water gushing through this natural aperture is black as pitch, save where the frenzied spray spurts upwards and dissolves on the rose-red crags of the outer walls. I wanted to get out my sketching pad there and then, but there was simply nowhere to sit.

Cherry amused himself by trying to harpoon a sea-snake in one of the pools. It was about five feet in length, of a grey colour striped with yellow, and once speared it twisted and bucked so violently that Cherry almost lost it. Much to his surprise it succeeded in biting him on the elbow, at which he swore loudly. Though I don't, as a rule, approve of bad language, it's rather a good sign in Cherry.

After examining the wound to make sure it wasn't deep, I told him to walk further out and bathe his arm in salt water. He hadn't been gone more than a few minutes when he let out a shout and I saw he was struggling with something caught between the rocks. He returned carrying a biscuit tin which he shook excitedly under my nose.

'There's something in it, Uncle Bill,' he said. 'Something heavy', and prising off the corroded lid he shook out another smaller tin with the likeness of Queen Victoria, much disfigured by sea water, stamped on the lid.

He spent the greater part of the walk back to West Bay trying to open the second box, without success. It was quite comical to watch him labouring away at the lid with his knife. I had earlier told him of the legend of buried treasure on the Island, gold and silver plate plundered from Peruvian churches, and I think he fully expected his little tin to contain some ancient map with a cross marking the spot.

When we reached our original landing place we were aghast to find a southerly swell rolling in and huge breakers bursting with a noise of thunder upon the beach. The natural pier was half torn away and we had a devil of a job getting a rope to the pram and swimming out with it to the whaler. Until it was my turn to cast off I sat on a crag munching a biscuit. Afterwards Birdie said my coolness had been an inspiration, and I hadn't the heart to disillusion him; the fact is, I'd got cramp.

All our specimens had to be left behind – Lillie's plants, my eggs, Oates's birds, Birdie's butterflies and spiders, as well as our guns, watches and notebooks. Oates was dreadfully put out at having to abandon the huge frigate, or man-of-war bird, he had slaughtered below the Ninepin, its wings measuring at least seventeen feet across at full spread. Worse, Seaman Murphy was considered too weak to fight the heaving seas. Atkinson elected to stay with him. Having dug out the rum and helped gather a pile of dead wood, we left them our outer clothing and plunged into the mountainous waves.

None of us slept well that night. The noise of the surf pounding on the beach was enough to waken the dead. The *Terra Nova* pitched like a cork; even Oates, a man with a cast-iron stomach, could be seen clinging to the rails in the small hours. We could see the glow from

Atkinson's fire and the sparks showering in the darkness.

Cherry had at last managed to open his tin, to find nothing more thrilling than a folded page torn from *The Times* newspaper of 1853 with a curious article to do with Gladstone encircled in faded ink. Coming home from the opera the great man had been accosted by a loose woman who had burst into tears and insisted on telling him of the several misfortunes which had led her to such a life. In the middle of this pathetic dialogue a man had stepped from the shadows and, addressing Gladstone by name, threatened to expose him in the *Morning Herald* unless he was given a sum of money, there and then, or a position as a clerk in Somerset House. The fact that the man's name was Wilson tickled everyone in the ward-room; I daresay the joke will run for weeks.

Still, it's interesting to wonder how such a salacious item from the past found its way to a deserted island. The Wilson in question was given twelve months hard labour. Teddy Evans has got it into his head that after his release the fellow signed on board some ship bound for the Cape, and either the vessel sank with all hands or Wilson died at sea and the captain slid him and his belongings overboard.

Oates, being more complex than Teddy, was intrigued by Gladstone rather than Wilson. He argued there was no smoke without fire, and what was a man in Gladstone's position doing walking home? 'I'll give him the benefit of the doubt as regards innocent involvement,' he said. 'But I won't excuse his stupidity.'

The next morning the sky was stormy and if anything the sea wilder than on the previous night. We could see the surf breaking over rocks at least sixty foot in height.

The wind was blowing in strong gusts right offshore, pushing the crests of the incoming waves into great veils of spray, bright with rainbows as the sun blazed through the clouds.

It was decided that Rennick, Bowers, Teddy Evans, Oates and myself should take the pram and the whaler in to rescue the castaways. With hindsight it was perhaps unwise of Teddy to insist on going with us. As commander of the ship it would have been unfortunate if he had come to any harm. In my capacity as chief of the scientific staff I too should have stayed behind; the truth is neither of us wanted to miss the fun.

The first idea had been to fire a rocket line to the edge of the cliff for Atkinson and the seaman to get a hold of. We realised at the second attempt that it was hopeless; the wind was too strong and the angle of the cliff all wrong. Birdie and Rennick got in the pram and somehow managed to get out a line to the shore for the gear to be taken off. It was our job to warn them of any big waves coming up behind. Time and again we bellowed 'Look out!', at which Birdie and Rennick rowed like the devil to pull away. I lost count of how often the line tore free. Everyone knows how the ocean swell moves in a regular rhythm, how at intervals two or three greater waves than usual come up one after the other, to be followed by a comparative calm during which, with skill, a boat can be swept ashore. Trouble was, we didn't want to be beached, for in such seas we'd never have got off again.

At last, during one of the brief lulls, Atkinson waded close enough to throw some of the gear into the pram, and some quarter of an hour after this triumph Rennick managed to drag the sick seaman aboard, Birdie leaping out into the surf to change places with him and steady the stern. The next moment the pram flew out in the backwash and Birdie disappeared under a torrent of water to emerge thirty long seconds later, twelve feet up on the rocks. I could see him scrambling for dear life away from the suck of a second huge wave that roared after him. The odd thing was, while his old brown tennis pumps were torn from his feet and never seen again, his treasured green hat remained firmly anchored to his head.

Evans and myself hauled the pram alongside the whaler and tumbled Rennick and Seaman Murphy over the gunnel. Then, despite my protests, Evans and Oates jumped into the pram and made again for the shore. By running down between waves Birdie got the guns, cameras and specimen cases aboard, at which we all cheered. Alas, we were premature, for the next instant a gigantic curl of water hurled the pram forward, Oates and Evans diving headlong into the boiling surf a split second before the following wave washed her high onto the rocks.

A pram is a marvellously buoyant little boat, yet such manoeuvres were immensely risky, and Rennick and I yelled ourselves hoarse ordering the men to abandon everything and return. To no avail; if I could have got my hands on Birdie I might have throttled him, so great was my anger. There were moments when the clap of the waves sounded like the beating of monstrous wings, and I feared that the silver bird of death had all along been searching for Birdie, not me, and would soon find him in the heaving depths.

For those involved in their battle with the sea, alternately submerged and clawing their way to the surface, time – as they afterwards recounted – passed with the swiftness of a disconnected dream. We who watched, expecting any moment that one or other would be drowned, remained in the grip of a nightmare which lasted six insufferable hours.

In the end the gear was lashed to buoys, thrown into the sea and somehow dragged into the whaler. The day's collection of ants, cockroaches and locusts, Birdie's fifteen different species of spider, and the blue sea crabs in which Atkinson later discovered a hitherto unknown nematode, were all but ruined by salt water. As for the eggs Cherry and I had so carefully gathered, we pitched the resulting fishy-smelling mess into the waves. My watch was lost, along with a leather wallet in which I kept a snapshot of my father. I daresay the latter will find its way back to the beach, where, God knows how many years hence, some other visitors may find it and view it with as much puzzlement as Cherry's page of *The Times*.

Surprisingly, apart from a quantity of gashed ankles and bruised ribs, no one was any the worse for wear. True, Atkinson and Seaman Murphy had spent a ghastly night kept awake by the sinister slithering of the land crabs and the melancholy cries of the numerous terns – a sound Murphy likened to the plucking of banjo strings – but one could tell from the sparkle in their eyes that such memories had been quite washed away in the exhilaration of their rescue.

Indeed everyone concerned behaved as if they'd just returned from a particularly lively party, and could have been mistaken, from their unnaturally loud voices and swaggering gait, for men in the grip of alcoholic stimulation. Oates, wild-eyed and in the middle of telling me how he had felt as weightless as a balloon – 'My dear Bill, you have no idea how I floated, yes floated, up the side of that damned cliff' – suddenly fell fast asleep across the ward-room table, a position he remained in for the next twelve hours.

Atkinson, Lillie and I stayed up all night in our separate workrooms, attempting to salvage what we could of the waterlogged specimens. I was uncomfortably aware that the scientific results of the *Discovery* expedition of 1901 had come under heavy criticism from the President of the Physical Society, who had gone so far as to suggest that Con should undergo a scientific court martial. Fortunately, it was the meteorological observations that had come most under fire – some error had occurred in the confusing of true and magnetic compass bearings – but I didn't want to take any chances and was determined to save as many of the birds as possible.

At sunrise, Birdie sought me out in my laboratory. He'd slept in his hat and it had buckled into the most extraordinary shape above his left ear. He also had a bruise across the bridge of his nose and looked altogether the pirate.

'Did I tell you about my Captain on the *Worcester*,' he said, looking down at the skeleton of the magnificent man-o'-war bird brought down by Oates. 'He taught me all I know about the skinning and preserving of birds ... not that it amounts to much.'

'You have mentioned him,' I said.

'He was a great man. He once said, not to me, but to a cadet who had got himself into debt, "Never be particular about money, unless it's not your own." I've never forgotten that.'

'I don't wonder,' I said. I was still angry with him for taking such risks the previous day. I had been going to tell him that only hours before we landed on South Trinidad, Campbell had told me he wanted him for the Eastern party set to explore Edward VII Land. He'd asked if I'd put in a good word with Con when we reached the Cape. I'd said I wouldn't, as I had every intention of recommending him for the shore party. After his recent reckless behaviour I didn't feel Birdie deserved to be acquainted with such proof of his capabilities, let alone his popularity.

He sensed I was fed up with him. 'Uncle Bill,' he said, looking as close to contrite as that ridiculous hat would allow, 'I expect we gave you a lot of worry yesterday. I do assure you we were never in any danger.'

'I'm going to have to revise my classification of the petrels,' I said. 'I had thought the black-breasted ones to be a different species from the white, but Cherry and I found them nesting together.'

'I never thought otherwise,' he replied. 'Black, white, yellow, we all have the same needs, though I've never considered the black-breasted kind to be the equal of the white,' and at that I couldn't help laughing, and so forgave him.

Later that day, we set sail in green seas, the southern rollers lifting us like a shuttlecock. I was still skinning in the laboratory when Birdie brought in my cocoa at ten o'clock. 'Do you know what, Uncle Bill?' he said. 'Don't let on to the other chaps, but I've just remembered it's my birthday.'

At that moment the ship wallowed sickeningly and shuddered; the monotonous chonk-chonk of the screw missed a beat. I slid sideways from the sink, my cocoa slopping onto the linoleum.

'Whoops,' Birdie shouted, putting out his hand to steady me, and then we were level again and I raised my mug and wished him all the luck in the world. It's a fine thing to know that wherever Birdie is, instability can only be temporary.

The Owner: Captain Robert Falcon (Con) Scott
March 1911

Having to sail on past Cape Crozier came as a frightful blow. I'd banked on establishing our winter quarters there, but it proved impossible to land owing to the swell. Nor could I risk waiting in hopes of calmer weather, for the *Terra Nova* had already consumed a dangerous amount of coal. All my plans and calculations had been made around this anchorage, it being in proximity to the Barrier, the volcano and the rookeries of two different kinds of penguins, thus satisfying the requirements of the geological, zoological and Polar factions of the expedition. We would have had an easy ascent of Mount Terror, a fairly easy approach to the Southern Road, ice for water, snow for the animals, good observation peaks, and so forth. In the old days the stench of guano from the rookeries used to turn my stomach, but when we were forced to steam away I wondered how I had ever found it offensive.

We pushed on beyond Cape Royds to the west coast of Ross Island. Here, in early January, we erected our base hut on the promontory that used to be known as the Skuary and since renamed Cape Evans. As soon as the hut was ready for occupation and all the stores and provision had been transferred safely from ship to shore, I took Campbell and Meares with a dog team to visit our old quarters at Hut Point.

It was a chastening experience. I suppose I'd expected to find everything as we'd left it seven years before, but some fool had forgotten to close a window, with the result that the interior had become a block of blue ice, in the middle of which were clamped several tins of ginger biscuits. We found half a loaf of bread with teeth marks in it stuck to the step of the door.

I'm inclined to think it must have been Shackleton's party of 1909 who left the window open, not us. After all, we had plenty of time, whereas Shackleton's lot had to bolt for the *Nimrod* in the lull of a blizzard. In the circumstances the securing of windows was the last thing on their minds, and then, of course, Shackleton was never a man for detail. All the same, I cannot understand the mentality of people so shallow, so lacking in foresight as to act in such a manner. Surely it's a mark of civilised human behaviour to leave a place in the condition one would wish to find it. One would think they had walked out of an hotel in some modern town, not a shelter in the most uninhabitable spot on earth, a refuge which could mean the difference between life and death to those who follow after. Such carelessness transgresses all the boundaries of common courtesy, and plunged me into depression. Which is possibly why I slept so badly: that and the fact there was something altogether strange about the place, something eerie, as though the past, which until now had remained as frozen as that flung-down loaf, had at last begun to thaw, releasing shades of days gone by. Although we were dead-beat after our strenuous march, all of us imagined we were disturbed by voices murmuring in the darkness, and Campbell swears he heard the crank of a gramophone handle and the cracked tones of Harry Lauder raised in song. I daresay all these noises were nothing more than the seals calling to one another; none the less, we passed an uncomfortable night. We felt better the next morning after we'd climbed up into the hills, possibly due to the sunshine. The glare warmed our bones and gave us energy. I was surprised by the lack of snow, the Gap and Observation Hill almost bare and a great bald slope on the side of Arrival Heights. Below Vince's cross we stumbled upon Ferrar's old thermometer tubes, sticking up as if they'd been rammed home yesterday.

I still can't come to terms with the futility of Vince's death. If I hadn't sent the men out to practise their sledging, if a blizzard hadn't blown up, if Hare, who later miraculously staggered home, hadn't been presumed lost, if the rest hadn't gone off on that suicidal search, if Vince had been wearing crampons – the ifs are endless and unrewarding. I might have become despondent all over again if something slightly more pressing hadn't struck home, namely that although the bays would freeze over early in March it would be a difficult thing to get the ponies across owing to the cliff edges at the side. I must admit it was something I hadn't taken into account.

The weather continuing fine, we sledged home in great style. I was astonished at the ease with which the dogs made progress, though I'm not yet entirely convinced of their usefulness, as their behaviour is so often erratic. For instance, they are, as a rule, perfectly good friends in harness, so long as they're pulling side by side; yet the second the traces get mixed up they turn savagely on one another and become raging, biting devils. There's something disquieting about this sudden naked display of brute instinct in tame animals. Also, they indulge in the disgusting habit of eating their own excrement. The ponies do the same, but as there's a great deal of grain in their feed the practice isn't so nauseating to observe. Meares is wonderfully informed about the handling of them, and tells me the secret of getting the best out of them on the march is to let them choose their own leader. This turns out to be less democratic than it sounds, as the leader is invariably the one who has terrorised the rest into acceptance by virtue of his being the strongest and most intelligent. He told me to keep a close eye on Osman, our best dog, and note how he ruled the pack. I did, and found it highly instructive. The slightest slackening off in pace in one of the other animals and Osman leapt sideways, nipped the offender in the shoulder, and was back in position in a trice, the chastisement administered without the least disturbance in the rhythm of the run. I couldn't help feeling there was something to be learnt from his example.

The welcome we received when we arrived back at Cape Evans was heartwarming, and I was delighted by the further improvements made to our already luxurious hut. The indefatigable Bowers had finished the annexe, roof and all. Not only does it provide ample storage space for spare clothing, sleeping bags, furs, provisions, etc., its extension gives complete protection to the entrance porch. The stables, a stout, well-roofed lean-to on the north side, were almost ready, and Titus Oates, in one of his rare outbursts of optimism, actually went so far as to say he thought the ponies would be exceedingly comfortable during the long winter ahead.

It really was splendid to see the manner in which everyone had chipped in and not wasted a moment. The scientists had got their instruments and work tables arranged, the differential magnetic cave was under way, the larder dug out and already stored with mutton and penguin. P.O. Evans was in the middle of overhauling and making adjustments to the sledges, and Gran, the young Norwegian brought along to teach us skiing, boasted of a concoction he had been working on, a mixture of vegetable tar, soft soap and linseed oil which, when applied to the ski runners, would stop them from freezing. Each man in his way is a treasure, and I can't help congratulating myself for picking them.

We now have a truly seductive home built on the dark sands of one of the spurs of Mount Erebus, and here at least, in the shadow of that mighty volcano, we shall be more than comfortably housed through the night-black days to come.

There was just one thing I felt would make for a happier ship. I had instructed Bowers to make cubicles for us all, so we could each fit up our own space, thus ensuring the tidier storing of personal belongings. This he had begun to do, but it immediately became apparent to me that the men would be more at ease if they were separated from the officers. With this in mind I got Bowers to build a bulkhead of provision cases between their space and ours. I'm quite sure the arrangement is to the satisfaction of officers and men alike. Whatever conversations take place on the other side of the divide, however audible and no matter of what purport or subject – it's possible I would have to make an exception in the plotting of mutiny – we are honour-bound to respect privacy and react, to all intents and purposes, as if stone deaf.

I had an amusing exchange with Clissold, the cook, before our evening meal. Ponting and I were coming back at sunset from photographing the *Terra Nova* held

fast to its wedge of ice on the outskirts of the Bay.
Ponting was fairly bubbling with enthusiasm, babbling
of the magnificence of the landscape, the glistening
bergs, the glaciers that ripple down beyond the bays to
thrust their gleaming snouts into the sea, the smoking
summit of Erebus amid its snow-capped peaks. Clissold
was relieving himself in an angle of the hut. He didn't
hear our approach because someone inside – most likely
Meares – had put an operatic record on the
gramophone. Clissold was standing there with closed
eyes, face raised to the heavens. We startled him, and he
gave a little grunt.

'It's only Mr Ponting and me, Clissold,' I said. 'We've
been down to look at the ship. Mr Ponting seems to
think this the most glorious spot on earth. What do you
say?'

'Well, sir,' he said, 'I don't know about glorious, but I
do feel at home.'

'Home?' said Ponting, taken aback. 'Are you a native
of the Scottish Highlands?'

'I was born and bred in the city, sir,' Clissold replied.
'And noise-ways I don't see much difference, what with
the seals honking and them birds screaming, not to
mention those blessed dogs.'

He'd prepared a most tremendous spread for our
evening meal – seal soup, roast mutton, redcurrant jelly,
asparagus. Usually Bill sits on my right-hand side, and I
was a little put out to find Teddy Evans had beaten him
to the post. He's such a robust character, waving his
arms about as he recounts his endless tall stories,
thumping the table to emphasise some point or other,
laughing at his own jokes, that an hour spent in such
close proximity leaves one exhausted. That being said,
his imitation of a Siberian sledge driver shouting out

commands to his dogs – he borrowed Clissold's knitted tea-cosy to wear on his head – was extremely comical, and at least it put an end to the previous vexed topic of the ponies and the motors.

While we were away at Hut Point, Day and Lashly had got the motors started, only to have them break down almost at once. Poor old Day is very morose about this, but he's such an excellent mechanic I'm quite sure the difficulties are only temporary. The ponies are a different matter; according to Oates no amount of tinkering will overcome their obvious defects. To my mind, rest and an increased diet will do wonders. We sat long at the table, all except Meares and Oates who spend a good deal of their time with the ponies. These two have struck up a great friendship, based, one imagines, on an unspoken communion, both of them being equally laconic.

I went for a short walk after supper, and came back via the stables. Through the window I could see Titus and Meares crouched over the blubber stove, pipes clamped in their mouths. The door was a little ajar to let out the smoke, and I was about to open it wider when I heard Oates say, 'We ought to buy the Owner a sixpenny book on transport', at which Meares laughed.

I was upset, of course, but then we all make disparaging remarks behind each other's backs and it simply isn't productive to take every scrap of overheard tittle-tattle to heart.

*

Towards the end of the month we said goodbye to all those on board the *Terra Nova*, which, under the command of Campbell, was preparing to sail 400 miles eastwards along the edge of the Great Ice Barrier to King Edward VII Land. She carried with her two geologists belonging to the shore party, and Wright, the physicist, who would be deposited further down the coast with the purpose of exploring the Western Mountains. I lent the latter group Petty Officer Evans, now something of an expert on sledging.

'Will we be gone long, then, sir?' he asked me, when I first told him he would be going.

'Several weeks, no more,' I replied, and noticed he looked rather downcast. 'Come, man,' I chided. 'Do you think I won't be able to manage without you?'

'I had thought I'd be here for my birthday, sir,' he said, and I couldn't help laughing.

'Birthdays,' I told him, 'are hardly our first priority.'

It was the aim of the depot party left behind – we had by this time established our first camp at the limit of open water six miles south of Glacier Tongue, close by our old *Discovery* hut – to lay as many provisions as possible at the furthest point on the Great Ice Barrier as we could manage before the winter closed in. Taking into consideration the infernal bad luck which has dogged me ever since leaving New Zealand, things are going forward as might be predicted – damned slowly and with unprecedented fluctuations in weather.

I fear I'm beginning to lose faith in the ponies. The storm that hit us twelve days out from Port Chalmers, and which nearly did for us all, has affected them terribly. I had hoped comfortable stabling and a few weeks rest on shore would have set them to rights, but their continuing feebleness fills me with alarm. Oates, a pessimist to his boots, doubts if they were ever in the best of health and never wastes an opportunity of listing their defects – Snippets: bad wind-sucker, slightly lame of forelegs; Victor: aged, narrow chest, knock-kneed, suffers from his eyes; Chinaman: ringworm above coronet on near fore, both nostrils slit up; Nobby: aged, goes with stiff hocks, spavin near hind, etc. As for Wearie Willie, Oates pronounces him a walking disaster.

It's obvious a serious mistake was made in the selection of them, but as Meares was assisted in his choice by 'Mumbo' Bruce, who joined him at Vladivostock, I can't be too forthright in laying blame. After all, Mumbo is my brother-in-law and I shouldn't want Kathleen to know he's let me down.

As always, Bill has been a tower of strength, reminding me that even though we've left the fittest of the animals behind at Cape Evans and only brought along what Titus Oates refers to as 'the crocks', we've still managed to get them to transport two good loads onto the Barrier. As for the dogs, they're doing better than I allowed for, and have run their first load almost two miles past this point to the site I've chosen for 'Safety Camp'. The name speaks for itself; in the unlikely event of the sea ice melting, taking with it part of the Barrier, this spot should remain intact.

Our short stint at sledging has already exposed weaknesses, not least in character. Atkinson has owned up to a badly chafed heel, an injury he hid until now in the misguided belief he would be letting the side down by complaining so early on in the march, with the result that the wound is now suppurating and he's unable to walk. I'm afraid I have very little sympathy for him, and am far more concerned about the ponies. The surface is appallingly soft and they're forever sinking past their hocks into the drift, something I hadn't bargained for. It would melt the hardest of hearts to watch them floundering and straining to get free, jumping with forelegs braced to take the cruel weight of the sledges, their struggles only serving to plunge them deeper, until, buried up to their shrunken bellies, they can move no more. Shackleton must have had the luck of the devil to have brought his animals thus far.

Also, and I find this astonishing, they appear to suffer from snow blindness, even though the skies are generally dismally overcast. Oates has suggested we dye their forelocks green to counter the glare.

Cherry-Garrard, who wears spectacles, is burdened with the same problem. Bill has found him a pair of *Discovery* glasses, made of wood with a cross slit in the middle, which he now uses with every sign of relief. It's inconvenient that the ponies don't have ears in the proper places.

Accordingly, I've revised my plans and from now on we shall travel by night and sleep by day. The sun never goes below the horizon, and though it is bitterly cold at all times, the so-called daylight hours are fractionally higher in temperature, and it seems sensible to allow the ponies to rest up in comparative warmth and slog it out in the bitter night, thus reducing exhaustion and eliminating the agony of snow glare.

Something happened yesterday which temporarily raised my expectations. Petty Officer Keohane discovered a set of snow-shoes under a provision box, and on fitting Wearie Willie with them he strolled around in the easiest manner possible. It was a miracle – even the pony seemed to think so, and kicked up his heels as if he was frolicking in a meadow. I immediately dispatched Meares and Bill with a dog team back to Cape Evans to fetch the other sets. It meant a wait in camp until their return, but I reasoned the delay would be more than justified once the rest of the ponies were similarly equipped.

Oates, of course, was unimpressed and gloomily remarked that any improvement was bound to be short-lived. It's his pessimistic opinion that the use of snow-shoes, like skis, requires practice. Unfortunately, I couldn't prove him wrong, because Bill eventually returned empty-handed. He'd found the sea ice gone between Glacier Tongue and the Cape and we are now cut off from our comfortable winter quarters!

On top of everything else, Atkinson's foot refuses to heal and I'm forced to go on without him. Worse, Tom Crean, a perfectly able man and one we can ill afford to spare, has to be left behind to act as nursemaid. Atkinson's carelessness in the matter of fitness has put an unfair load on the rest of us and I've had to reorganise.

Still, in spite of all our setbacks and the continuing wretched surface conditions, my spirits rise at the thought of being on the move again. Inactivity always leads to introspection, and I'm simply no good when I'm not doing something. It will be splendid to fall asleep utterly exhausted from a long, strenuous slog.

*

Each day begins very much like the last. A little before 9 pm we struggle out of our sleeping bags, light up the primuses and cook breakfast. Some two hours later, having been ready and raring to go an hour since, I shout to Titus, 'How are things?', and he shouts back, calmly enough, 'Fine, sir, fine.'

The tents are struck, the rugs come off the horses, the sledges are loaded, the dogs wrestled into submission – and still I wait. Attempting to get everyone off on time is like trying to spoon treacle back into a tin with a feather.

The monotony of our routine makes for slackness, and inside my head I'm forever giving lectures on how we must buck up and come to the realisation we're not on a picnic.

In these temperatures the energy derived from hot food soon evaporates if one is forced to hang about, and the few who have stirred themselves into readiness suffer for the tardiness of the many. It's difficult to hold one's temper in check, and often I positively have to clench my jaw to stop myself from roaring with fury. Saintly old Bill merely smiles patiently and stomps up and down to keep his feet from freezing. Bowers, oblivious both to the delay and the cold, is here, there and everywhere, checking loads, adjusting traces, consulting his notebook. The dogs leap in alarm as the crust of the snow snaps beneath their paws. The sun, blurred by wreathing drift, casts a pale, shadowless light.

At last, past midnight, we get under way. Finnesko can't get a grip on the slippery surface and we fall down like inebriates. At first, from embarrassment, we used to utter curses, engage in comic banter; now, dumbly picking ourselves up, one hour succeeding another, one foot following the other, we concentrate on drawing breath against the icy wind. Above our heads, weaving among the panting exhalations, swirl pictures of home, beloved faces, food.

At the end of the march – under these adverse conditions we're barely averaging ten miles a day – I blow my whistle, and at the blast Birdie and Bill wheel to the left, Oates and I come to a halt behind, and the rest advance ahead. We are thus drawn up into camp formation, and in less than ten minutes the ponies are out of harness, the tents up, the cookers in place and the hoosh on the simmer. The dog teams, who have set off after us, try to time their arrival to coincide with ours. They have a pretty cold wait before catching up with us, but as they're so much quicker than the ponies there doesn't seem any better way of arranging things.

Before we eat we build snow walls for the ponies. This was my idea, and at first there were quite a few sniggers behind my back; once they were up and everyone could see the benefit, it was a different story. Now it's one of the first tasks Titus Oates sets himself when we make camp.

I suffer pretty monotonously from stomach pains, and spend a good quarter of an hour after supper walking about battling the wind both without and within. I've always believed my gastronomic problems were due to bolting my food in order to get on with the more pleasurable business of smoking, but Kathleen has half persuaded me the trouble is down to undigested conflicts.

According to her, the difficulty my stomach has in processing food is directly linked to an inability to express my feelings. Fortunately, this was my nurse's fault, not mine, for in failing to comfort me when I cried she apparently conditioned me to regard any display of emotion as useless, thus shifting my natural sense of outrage from heart to belly. Which is why my infant son Peter has only to let out a squawk for him to be instantly picked up and petted.

When Kathleen was pregnant she sometimes slept out in the back garden. She told my mother, who would have been happier left in ignorance, that our unborn child needed to lie under the stars. I'm afraid my mother thinks Kathleen too Bohemian for her own good, let alone mine. I must admit that on the rare occasions I've been left with the boy and he's cried I've been shaken by the anguished expression on his yawling face; yet when I jiggled him up and down as instructed, the effect was disappointing. Kathleen said it was because he didn't know me. When I discussed the matter with Bill, who is, after all, a medical man, he was fairly scathing, holding that children mostly wept from anger and an unconscious desire for discipline; he is, of course, childless.

We're five to a tent at the moment, and if the going hasn't been too hard we have a good chat once we've got out our tobacco ration. Bill, no longer a serious smoker, indulges in a cigar, Teddy Evans favours cigarettes and I enjoy my pipe, though I'll smoke anything on offer. It's wonderful to get up a good fug after the misery of the march, and astonishing how quickly resentments vanish in the wake of that first, heavenly inhalation. I'm afraid Cherry-Garrard weeps from the resulting irritation to his eyes, but he's a splendid sport and never complains. He obviously worships Bill, who, in his turn, is tremendously patient with him and spends hours teaching him the ropes, how to keep his foot-gear dry and so forth. As a result Cherry is shaping up awfully well and will be a great asset to us next year.

What conversations we have! There's scarcely a country under the sun which one or other of us hasn't travelled in, nor any subject, ranging from the scientific to the philosophical, on which we don't hold an opinion. We discuss the medieval ramparts of Aigues Mortes, the pronunciation of ancient Greek, the extraordinary aspirations of women and the working-class in our present society, the pernicious influence that modern inventions – motorised transport, the use of balloons for meteorological observation, sail versus steam – may or may not have on future explorations, and whether the power wielded by Jesuits in the sixteenth century was ultimately a *good thing*. This last debate, initiated this morning by Bill, bored me. I took off my shoes, got into my sleeping bag, knocked out my pipe and ordered the others to do the same. I truly love Bill, but when he starts bleating on about Ignatius Loyola I become irritated. If Kathleen were here she'd probably suggest it's because I can't stomach him admiring someone else.

*

The condition of three of the weakest ponies, Teddy Evans's Blossom, Keohane's Jimmy Pig and Forde's Misery, gradually worsened. Misery was reduced to scarcely more than skin and bone, and Jimmy Pig went lame. It was very worrying, and I could have done without Oates's consistently gloomy predictions. We had quite a bust-up when we made one of our half-march halts.

I was foolish enough to tell Bill, within Oates's hearing, that I was thinking of sending Evans and the two men back to Safety Camp with the sick ponies.

'We don't want to lose them,' I said. 'And the poor things have suffered enough.'

'Is that wise?' he asked, at which Oates burst out, 'No, it damn well isn't. They won't last out the return march.'

'They will with lighter loads,' I said.

'They're hardly carrying anything as it is,' he persisted. 'It would be far better to increase the loads and push them on until they drop. Then next year they can be fed to the dogs. That way at least their suffering will have been of some damn use.' He addressed Bill, by the way, not me – he knows Bill can't stand confrontation.

'I've had enough of this cruelty,' I told him. 'Personally, it makes me sick.'

'Then I'm afraid you'll regret it, sir,' he drawled, regarding me in that ironical way of his.

'Regret it or not,' I retorted, 'I've made up my mind,' and there and then I informed Evans and the others they would be returning the following night.

At the end of the march the atmosphere in the tent was somewhat strained, and not improved by Cherry-Garrard putting his foot in it with some rambling tale concerning a pony he'd owned as a boy. It had something to do with how he'd gone for a ride wearing his best clothes and how the animal had stalled at a fence, pitching him headlong into a cattle trough. Normally the anecdote would have been received with the suppressed yawns it deserved, but of course on this occasion it gave Titus the opportunity to remind us of the differences between family 'pets' and 'working' animals.

The word 'working' was emphasised in such a sarcastic tone that I nearly got into a spat with him for a second time, and would have done if Bill hadn't butted in with the comment that there was no such thing as purely reproductive recollection. The ensuing argument had a soothing, yet curiously exhilarating effect and centered much round the dead having more reality for men than the living.

Bill held that the reputations of the remembered dead, from the insignificant mannikin to the most illustrious subject, underwent a change from the very moment of departure. Temporal existence ended, the imaginative faculty of posterity took over. The man who had died in battle, or in the pursuance of some purely personal goal, instantly became the brave hero who had perished for the glory of his country.

At this point Bowers came in from outside, having been attending to all those things none of us realised needed doing. He really is a most exceptional fellow – while we wear thick Balaclavas and wind hoods, all he had on his head was that misshapen hat. He'd overheard Bill's last remark and vigorously agreed with him, maintaining that the living, out of a natural fear of death, needed to attach lofty motives to earthbound reactions, and that an act of so-called courage was merely a spontaneous response, dictated by upbringing, to a sticky situation.

I must say I surprised myself by calling them both cynics. 'Bravery is a conscious act of discipline,' I asserted. 'And as far as I'm concerned there are worse things than dying. Cowardice for one.'

Bill misunderstood me and proposed that many men welcomed death, at which Titus and I cried out with one voice that he was talking morbid rot. After that he and I were civil to each other.

I did consider telling him I regretted we'd had words earlier, that I understood his opposition to the return of the ponies was conducted in good faith, even that future events might well prove him to be right, but I didn't. Justifying my actions would have been simply no good for morale. Like it or not, and God knows, half the time I don't, someone has to take the decisions – along with the consequences.

That night's march was begun in moonshine, though it soon clouded over. I didn't like the threatening aspect of the sky. The going, as usual, was wretchedly soft; even the dogs seemed to be labouring. For some unknown reason Osman had been disposed, in a not entirely bloodless coup, and Rabchick appeared to have taken over as leader.

These surfaces have taught Meares a valuable lesson, namely that he must rely on his own two feet. Until we began the depot laying I fear he had but a hazy notion of what conditions would be like and rather imagined he would ride the sledges in the Siberian fashion.

After dragging ourselves no more than four miles, by which time the wind had veered ominously from south to north and the temperature dropped to minus sixteen, Teddy Evans said his pony could go no further, and we made camp.

The blizzard hit us just before dawn, and for the next fifty-two hours we were laid up in the tents. It wasn't so bad for us, for once into our sleeping bags it was easy to ignore the hell blowing outside. When one realises there is absolutely nothing one can do about it, it's astonishing the number of hours one can doze through. The dogs too were perfectly comfortable; they merely dug themselves into holes and lay on top of one another. It was the ponies who again suffered the most, though Oates and Birdie were in and out night and day attending to them.

As soon as the blizzard had blown itself out we said goodbye to Evans and his party and struck off south, the sun circling low on the horizon. We struggled under puffy pink clouds sailing in a sky of deepest grey. The drift froze on the sledge runners and we were constantly stopping to scrape them free. After only an hour or so of this drudgery Gran, who was leading Weary Willie, dropped behind, so far back that the dog teams caught up. Suddenly Oates and I, who were ahead, heard the most tremendous commotion – barking, whinnying, men shouting.

We hurried back and met Meares who said the dogs had attacked Weary Willie. He'd fallen down and they were on him in an instant, sinking their teeth into shoulder and throat, raking his belly with their claws as if to disembowel him. Gran had broken his ski stick and Meares his dog whip in beating them off.

When I got to the scene Weary Willie was on his feet again, legs splayed out, head hanging low, the dogs still snarling horribly, eyes watchful for an advantage, their silvery breath making circles in the frosty air. Willie had given as good as he got, and two of his attackers were bleeding badly. The whole episode was sickening and confirmed my opinion of the unreliability of the dogs. When we moved off we left a trail of blood dripping scarlet blotches on the snow.

After lunch, Wilson, Bowers and I went and fetched Wearie Willie's load. It was far heavier than that of the other ponies, and obviously this was the cause of Willie falling down in the first place. I was fuming at such carelessness. I blamed Gran, Oates, Meares – especially Meares. 'He's all very well in his way,' I accused, 'but he's far too slack in his attitude.'

'If you say so,' said Bill.

'It was apparent to me from the moment I joined the ship at the Cape. Do you remember him coming up on deck in pyjamas? And his surprise when I bawled him out for it?'

'Yes,' Bill said. 'I do remember.'

'I can't stand his disgusting habit of shaving the soles of his feet in the tent.'

'Yes,' said Bill. 'It is pretty hard to take.'

I raged on in this manner almost all the way back. Bill bore the brunt of it – Bowers had distanced himself by trudging ahead – nodding, murmuring agreement, occasionally tut-tutting in sympathy, until, the tents coming into sight, he cut me short. 'I imagine,' he said, 'you've covered everything pretty thoroughly. I don't feel it will do the slightest good to repeat any of it to the others. What's done is done.' I took his advice, but my God, it gave me a stomach ache.

Two days later we built our last depot at One Ton camp. In the space of twenty-two days, twelve of us, with twenty-six dogs and eight ponies, had managed to cross the 79th Parallel and deposit a ton of stores 150 miles distance from Cape Evans. I would have liked to have pressed on further, but the ponies were done in, the dogs beginning to slow down, and so were we, some of us more than others. Meares had become incapacitated with an ingrowing toe-nail, and Oates's nose showed signs of frostbite.

We planted a black flag firmly on the top of One Ton depot, packed the sides of the cairn with biscuit boxes, so that the tin should reflect the sun, and turned back.

Twenty-four hours later we were laid up in another blizzard, only this time we were prepared for it and the ponies were better protected. All the same, I was desperately worried about the sick animals sent back with Evans, and as soon as the weather improved, Bill, Cherry-Garrard, Meares and myself dashed for home with a dog team, leaving the others to follow with the 'crocks'.

I won't dwell on what happened on the way – sufficient to say the dogs fell into a crevasse and we nearly lost the lot. They were twisting on their traces for an hour or more, and some undoubtedly suffered internal injuries. Even while they dangled, howling in agony, they still continued to bite and tear at one another. Such uncivilised behaviour went some way towards dulling compassion for their plight.

On reaching Safety Camp I was relieved to see Evans

and the others safe and sound. Alas, two of the three ponies had died on the way, Jimmy Pig being the sole survivor. The thing was, there was no sign of either Crean or Atkinson, not even a note. After a hot meal, Meares and I went to Hut Point in the hopes of finding them there.

A mystery awaited us; although the old *Discovery* Hut was now clear of ice and had evidently been lived in – there were socks hanging rigid on the line above the stove – it was deserted. A pencilled note on the door said there was a bag inside containing mail, but there wasn't. I concluded Atkinson had returned to Safety Camp and we'd somehow passed each other on the way.

Back we went, and I almost wished we'd perished in the attempt, for Atkinson and his woeful bag were indeed there, and the news, conveyed in a letter penned by Campbell, was worse than anything I could have imagined. Amundsen's intentions, hinted at in that fateful telegram I received in Melbourne, were now out in the open. Campbell had sailed into the Bay of Whales to find that the Norwegians had got there before him.

It was a shattering blow to my hopes; indeed we were all fearfully affected. I turned in early and lay miserably in my sleeping bag. Usually the camp noises continue into the small hours; people calling out to one another; the clatter of cooking utensils; voices raised in good-humoured argument – so much so that often I've had to give the order for silence. But that night the men spoke in whispers and even the dogs ceased to bark.

At midnight Bill brought a mug of cocoa to my tent. 'I thought you could do with this,' he said. 'I knew you wouldn't be asleep. None of us are.'

I told him I thought Amundsen's behaviour was absolutely appalling. 'His duplicity, his lack of sportsmanship leaves me shuddering with disgust. All the while he was telling the world he was going north he was in fact proceeding south, although he knew perfectly well through newspaper reports what my own plans were.'

'Drink it while it's hot, Con,' Bill urged. 'It will help you sleep.'

'You realise he's a whole degree further south than we are,' I shouted. 'And he's got over a hundred dogs. It's quite obvious he intends to make a dash for the Pole.'

'Yes,' Bill said. 'It certainly looks like it.'

'Goddammit, Bill, he's not interested in science. He just wants to make a race of it.' I was so incensed I actually ground my teeth.

'Now look here,' Bill argued, 'we've got the ponies and we've got the motor transport.'

'Yes,' I retorted, 'and owing to carelessness in unloading, the best damn motor we had is at this moment lying at the bottom of McMurdo Sound.'

'That's unfair,' Bill protested. 'It was on your orders that Campbell had it shifted.'

'Even Lashly's lost faith in them. When they did manage to coax the blessed things to start they broke down five minutes later. As for the ponies ...'

'There was more than one person who spoke out against the folly of squandering hundreds of pounds on machines,' Bill said. 'Nansen among them.' And now he, too, was shouting. 'May I remind you that when you asked his advice, he said dogs, dogs, and dogs again.' After this outburst he stalked off.

The heat went out of me. Sweet Bill is so rarely stung into apportioning blame where it's due that I hadn't a leg to stand on. I plucked the reindeer hairs from my mouth and gulped down the cocoa. I trusted he'd come back. When he did, half an hour later, he squatted down on his haunches and said earnestly, 'I apologise for losing my temper, but I really can't stand what amounts to whining ... not from you, of all people.'

'My dear fellow,' I said, and I did feel contrite. 'You were absolutely right to speak as you did. It's just that we've had such damnable bad luck ... lack of money ... not being able to land where we wanted, the failure of the ponies, the ice breaking up, those blasted motors.'

'None of it is important,' he said. 'None of that matters.'

'The whole expedition is terribly unwieldy for one man to run. Perhaps we were too ambitious ... perhaps I should have brought more dogs and less ponies.'

'Now look here,' Bill said, 'forget the dogs, forget the ponies, the weather, the inadequate funding, and all the rest of it. Concentrate on what counts. First and foremost, remember this was always meant to be a scientific expedition, not just a conquest of the Pole. That's the thing to cling on to. And above all, remember you have the best set of fellows under you a man could ever wish for. In the end, that's what matters.'

I think I dreamt all night, a kaleidoscope of disturbing images – someone reading to me from a book full of pictures of giant birds; Kathleen running away down an embankment beside a river; the pony I rode to school cantering across a meadow, flanks streaming blood; my father zigzagging along an avenue of birches, weeping. The last thing I properly remembered was dear, dead Archie raising his gun to shoot his first wood pigeon. The explosion, tearing the trees apart, jolted me wide awake and turned into the furious yapping of quarrelsome dogs.

I ran out of the tent and looked for Bill. He was over by the sledges, attending to the runners. 'By Jove, Bill,' I cried, seizing him by the arm. 'We should have taken them. There's no law down here.'

'Taken whom?' he asked, looking blank.

'Amundsen,' I said. 'Amundsen and the rest of his damned crew. *We're* the law. We should have fought it out, with guns if need be.'

He moved away, forcing me to follow him. 'Look here,' he hissed. 'You must pull yourself together.' He was terribly shocked. He marched off, footsteps cracking in the snow, speaking over his shoulder in a furious whisper, urging me to lower my voice.

He told me afterwards that my suggestion that we should abandon civilised practices and take the Norwegians by force half convinced him I'd lost my mind. Apparently Forde and Crean were standing only a dozen paces from us. I'd been aware of no one in the whole white world but him.

I know I was not myself, but I don't doubt if Oates and Birdie had been there they would have backed me up to the hilt. Unlike Bill, who's been trained to dissect the dead, we three have been schooled to provide the corpses.

I came to sanity under Bill's tuition. He wisely said I must continue as if nothing had happened, as if Amundsen didn't exist. It was unthinkable that our scientific projects should be sacrificed in a vulgar scramble to reach the Pole.

Bill's definition of vulgarity hardly meets my own, but I said what he wanted to hear. What other choices did I have? 'You're right,' I agreed, 'as always, you're absolutely right. We must go on, without fear or panic, and do our best for the honour of our country.' I sounded convincing.

In the circumstances I couldn't stay in one place. The next morning I organised a party to set off for Corner Camp with the double purpose of taking out more stores and meeting Bowers and Oates. We man-hauled, as I was damned if I was going to travel with those bloodthirsty dogs. I didn't let on, but I fancied there was something broken in me, some spring that no longer worked. When we halted, even my pipe tasted of ashes.

There were five pony walls in evidence at Corner Camp, a sure sign that Birdie and Oates had passed that way. We left six weeks' stores for men and animals and made our return. A bit of a blizzard blew up and raged for two days, but I refused to call a permanent halt. There were one or two murmurs at this, particularly from Atkinson and Teddy Evans. They really must learn that the more beastly the conditions, the harder the slog, the better prepared we shall be for the journey next year.

Our reunion with Bowers and Oates at Safety Camp was hardly a joyful occasion. Meares, on hearing their approach, had run from the tent – apparently clad in nothing but his underpants – and blurted out the news concerning Amundsen.

Bowers was very cut up – mostly on my account, which I found irritating. He launched into a passionate attack on the Norwegians, calling Amundsen a rotter, a sneak, and a good few other names. 'If there's any justice,' he said, 'once the rest of the world gets to hear of his deceitful behaviour, he'll be condemned by all right-thinking men.' His voice shook, and his eyes were so full of pity I might have been a household pet he'd discovered mangled in some accident.

'It makes not the slightest difference to me,' I replied. 'I shall proceed as if he wasn't there, and I advise you to do the same.'

He went quite red in the face, and I could have kicked myself for sounding so cold with him. It's to be regretted that the best of me, the part that recognises both the horror and beauty of destiny, remains submerged. When things go wrong – and God knows they do that with unfailing regularity – while outwardly I exhibit all the signs of a man in the grip of bad temper, underneath I'm actually going through a healing, if melancholy, acceptance of forces beyond my control. However, the process is so debilitating that I'm forced to assume a reserve I'm far from feeling, otherwise I wouldn't be able to function.

Some time later Bill came and told me the men were very low. The recent blizzard, coming on top of everything else, had much reduced them and they were all feeling the cold. 'Morale is rock-bottom,' he warned. I decided the only course was to move immediately to Hut Point.

Bill advised against it. He said it was too dangerous, as the sea ice was possibly breaking up. I'm afraid I had to remind him who was in command. I hated doing it, but really, if every time I give an order every Tom, Dick and Harry feels free to put his oar in, we'll get nowhere. I apologised afterwards.

The sledges were three or four feet under drift, and it was late afternoon before the dog teams got away. I'd planned to follow with three groups of ponies, my party to start last and then spurt ahead of the others. Tom Crean, Cherry-Garrard and Bowers got off all right, but when we removed the blankets from Weary Willie his condition proved worse than I could possibly have imagined – ribs bursting through the skin, an open gash on the shoulder from his brush with the dogs, a continual tremble wracking the poor beast from nose to tail. Oates was all for putting a bullet through him on the spot.

'I think not,' I said. 'We should give him his chance,' and I gave the order for Bill and Meares to start.

'We ought to finish him off, sir,' persisted Oates. 'It would be a great mistake for us to fall behind the others, the weather being so bad. He won't last five yards.'

'We'll coax him along,' I said.

It was a losing battle. When Oates and I tried to get Willie to move, without a load and untethered, he instantly fell down. No matter what we did, he wouldn't rise; a dreadful film of defeat dulled his eyes.

'You might as well leave him to me and Anton, sir,' Oates said. 'We can manage between us. You and Gran go on ahead.'

'I'll decide when I shall leave,' I said, as evenly as I could manage. I believe Oates thought I was acting out of a sentimental regard for dumb animals. He's a man of few words, and those not often complimentary, and so comfortable with himself – and why not, he's wealthy enough – as to be incapable of stooping to self-doubt. I can't pretend we hit it off; yet I feel there's mutual respect. I take him for a good soldier, and what might be termed a strenuous man, and I expect, with hindsight, it'll come home to him that I have to be the one to call the shots. In the meantime he can go on scoring points off me.

We hoisted the pony up by brute force and propped him against the snow wall. He would have fallen again if I hadn't crouched down and supported his shrunken belly with my back. Anton, the Russian groom, boiled up a mash and he and Titus literally spooned the stuff down the poor thing's throat. Several times I attempted to ease myself from under him, only to feel the instant buckling of his knees. A curious thing, there was no smell to him at all, no odour of harness or blood or fetid breath, nor any stench of waste, though the snow beneath him was stained sepia with urine. The scant hair on his withered flanks, far from being rank with sweat, scraped dry as corn stubble against my wrist.

I crouched there for some time, looking down at my own footsteps jumbled in the snow. I thought of the accident to the dogs on our way back to Safety Camp. Two had dropped out of the traces and landed on a snow bridge some seventy feet below, and when we'd hauled the others up I went down on the alpine rope and managed to rescue them. I wondered how long it would be before one or other began to sicken from the ordeal. Those dangling in the crevasse must have suffered ruptures; three had already started passing blood.

Had I perhaps been foolish to risk my own neck? I had fallen from a rope thirty years before, in the birch avenue at Outlands. My father had climbed a tree and slung a rope over for Archie and me to swing on. It was one of his good days. He took first go, swirling round, feet kicking up the gravel path, Archie thumping him on the shoulderblades so that he twisted again, round and round, the three of us wild with excitement. Then he said he'd give me sixpence if I could shin to the top of the rope. Half way up I could see the house in the distance, the sun glinting on the conservatory glass, and I waved one hand in case my mother should be watching, and fell. I was so giddy with laughter I dropped with my mouth open and knocked out a tooth.

The daydream was so real I forgot where I was; as though on that childhood rope I swung out and up from under Weary Willie, at which the wretched animal collapsed, although this time he seemed to make some effort to scramble upright. I couldn't bear it. I left Oates and Anton to do what they could, and walked about.

Those who envisage this place as nothing more than a godforsaken plateau of ice and snow are mistaken. For one thing, there are outcrops of jet-black rock about which the wind blows so fiercely that the snow can never settle; and for another, the ice, being subject to reflections of sun and sea, is never purely white but tinged with rose and cobalt-blue and every shade of violet, the whole set against skies, day or night, that run through all the colours of the spectrum. Tonight there were lowering clouds of deepest purple, a sure indication of worse weather to come.

There is nothing on earth so vast, so glorious, as the southern heavens. In the· ordinary world a man measures himself against the height of buildings, omnibuses, doorways; here, scale blown to the four quarters, he'd be a fool not to recognise he's no more significant than a raindrop on an ocean. Standing there, it seemed irrelevant where Amundsen was – we were both cut down to size.

That being said, I was nevertheless seriously alarmed about the ponies. At this rate their numbers would be drastically reduced before we even started the Polar journey. Jimmy Pigg had left in a pitiful state, as had Bowers's animal. I'd underestimated the effect blizzards could have on them and, unless their condition miraculously improves, it almost certainly means a late start at the end of the year. We never encountered such frightful weather on the 1901 expedition – not during the month of March. It's surely unprecedented, and I don't see how I could have taken it into account.

We watched over Wearie Willie into the small hours. It was bitterly cold. Anton squatted on his haunches and rocked himself to sleep. Gran had turned in. Since the news of his countryman's arrival he's lost some of his bounce, which is all to the good. I don't hold his nationality against him. He's a tolerable enough chap, apart from being somewhat lazy and exhibiting a marked aversion to soap and water.

Oates kept me awake by asking questions about Ross, Franklin, Crozier and the rest of the bunch. His interest centred on the fate of Franklin's expedition, which had sailed north in 1845 and never returned. An investigation, paid for by Franklin's wife, had uncovered the unpalatable fact that a few crew members had survived, though not for long, by eating the numerous dead.

'I think I can accept that,' Oates said. 'One should never underrate the instinct for survival.'

'Under certain conditions,' I said, 'I suspect instinct is the one thing left functioning.'

'If we should get into such a pickle,' he said, 'I would prefer to shoot myself.' His face in the light of the lantern, skin pitted blue from the smallpox, appeared curiously young. For once, his eyes expressed uncertainty.

'In the unlikely event of its being necessary,' I said, 'we have more up-to-date methods. Bill has opium and morphia.'

'Damn it, no,' he said. 'I want to be in control. I don't want to drift into death.'

He's a solitary by nature, and a nihilist, which is why he ordered his men to abandon their positions and leave him to play the hero in the gully in South Africa. It's easy to be brave when the only life in jeopardy is one's own. Although it's never been my lot to have that singular experience, I can well imagine the surge of well-being such a sacrifice can bring.

The pony died. Anton set about the grisly job of chopping it up for the dogs. Oates didn't crow over me. If he were less confident and I more sure, we might be friends.

We set off on skis early in the morning. Above us the wind blew the heaped clouds along rivers of gold and crimson light. A quarter of a mile from the Barrier edge the sky darkened and the broken shapes of huge floes jostled on the distant horizon. I thought it an optical illusion – one often gets such mirages – but as we drew nearer we found to our horror that they were real. The sea was a seething mass of floating chunks of Barrier ice. A mere six hours earlier we could have walked to the Hut on sound sea ice.

Everything fitted into place – the decline of the ponies, the death of Wearie Willie, the calamitous fall of the dogs into the crevasse. Let those who believe in random happenings, Caesar among them, carry on believing the fault lies in ourselves; nobody will ever convince me that the stars don't play a part in it. My heart sank at the thought of the fate of the advance parties.

Retreating, we marched parallel to the edge until we discovered a working crack. We dashed over this and increased pace as much as possible, not slackening until we were in a line between Safety Camp and Castle Rock. I took out the glasses and made out two specks moving in the direction of Pram Point. Hastening on, we met Meares and Bill, who greeted us with relief as they'd feared we were lost. Bill, disregarding orders, had taken a different route, and on climbing Observation Hill had

spotted ponies adrift on the sea ice. He had thought it
was our group.

We put up the tent and brewed a hot drink. We were
all terribly cast down, though Bill did his usual best. He
was of the opinion that Teddy Evans, starting so much
earlier, might possibly have got through. And if it was
Bowers out there, why then he was such an indomitable
little fighter he was bound to survive. Gran pretended
to believe him. Oates didn't say a word. He sat with
slumped shoulders, staring fixedly at the flame of the
primus.

'Come now,' I said, attempting a cheerfulness I was
far from feeling, 'Bill's right. Dear old Birdie is
well-nigh indestructible.'

'There's every possibility he took a different route,'
Bill said, backing me up.

'Dear old Birdie,' Oates said, 'would stick to the route
he was told to take. Dear old Birdie's a stickler for
following orders, even when they're given by a bloody
fool.' Then he left the tent.

Bill was shocked on my account. He was all for going
after Titus and having it out with him.

'No,' I said. 'Leave him. I imagine he's only putting
into words what the rest of you think.'

At that moment Oates let out a shout, and on rushing
outside we saw him pointing at a solitary figure walking
in the direction of Safety Camp. Gran went off on skis to
intercept, and brought back Crean, completely done in
and far from coherent. As far as we could gather the ice
had broken up all around while they were camped for
the night. One pony had disappeared. They had packed
with great haste and jumped from floe to floe, pulling
the horses after them.

'The sea was like a cauldron,' Crean said. 'And them

killer whales were all about us, rearing their ugly snouts. We somehow got near to the Barrier edge, but when we tried to climb up bits kept breaking off and we couldn't get a purchase. Lieutenant Bowers said one of us would have to go for help, so I left him and Mr Gerrard behind and went off sideways, jumping and scrambling until I comes to a heftier piece of ice which drifted closer in. Then I managed to get off and up.'

'Well done, Crean,' I said. 'You're a resourceful chap. I can't tell you how happy it makes me to have you safe.'

'Them whales, sir,' he repeated, shuddering. 'Them murderous whales.'

We lost no time in getting to Safety Camp to pick up rope and provisions. Marching cautiously in a half circle, we approached the ice edge. I'm not sure I'm a full-time Christian, but every step of the way I prayed to God I should find my men alive. To my intense joy I caught sight of Birdie and Cherry almost immediately. I was so relieved I found it damn near impossible to blink back the tears. We got out the rope and dragged them onto the Barrier. There was no time for anything but a heartfelt handshake all round before commencing the laborious task of salvaging the sledges and equipment.

We worked into the small hours, and just as I'd decided we could now attempt to haul up the three ponies the ice began to shift again. Exhausted, we could do nothing more for them beyond attaching an anchor line to the floe and throwing down a quantity of fodder. Then we turned into our sleeping bags. None of us slept.

The next morning we found the anchor had drawn and there was no sign of the ponies. Bowers begged we should at least go on a little further in the faint hope of finding them alive. We followed the edge for some three quarters of a mile without result, and were just about to turn back when Bowers caught sight of them through the binoculars.

It wasn't too difficult to reach them, and we decided they should be rushed over the floes in a last attempt at rescue. We were worn out, don't forget, and more than a little overwrought – we tried to leap the first pony across, but even as his front hooves left the ice the gap widened and he plunged into the water. There was no way we could pull him out, and yet it was unthinkable to leave him there. Oates showed Bowers the quickest way to end its misery. 'Now,' he shouted, grasping the animal by its mane to hold its head steady, 'Strike hard!' and Bowers sank the pickaxe into the middle of its forehead.

I fought back nausea and concentrated on digging footholds for the other two ponies. We got one out, and thought we had the other; at the last moment it jumped short and slipped into the water, the killer whales rising all around, Oates hollering like a madman in an effort to scare them off. He and Birdie managed to haul the poor beast onto the floe. Birdie straddled its back and fought to yank it upright, but it couldn't rise from its knees.

I don't think any of us were in our right minds. None of us will forget that nightmare scene – the ice chunks heaving in the black water amidst the bucking whales, Birdie grotesquely riding that dying pony, Titus swinging the pickaxe against a sky the colour of blood.

*

We are now languishing in the old *Discovery* Hut waiting for the sea ice to freeze over. It's hardly as comfortable as the one at Cape Evans, yet snug enough for all that. Bowers, having wrought miracles out of empty kerosene cans and firebricks, has constructed a stove connected to the old pipe. Within days, such is his nature, he decided it would soon exhaust our supply of firewood and redesigned the whole thing to run on blubber. We boil our cocoa on a primus and stew or fry on the stove. It makes for a lot of smoke, but it generates a lot of heat. Not a day passes without Bill remarking to me, or me to him, on the marvellous qualities possessed by Birdie.

We're all right for food. What with sugar, salt, raisins, lentils and sardines, etc., we shan't starve. Indeed, some of our number are in danger of putting on weight and have to be chivvied into taking exercise, Teddy Evans, Meares and Gran being the worst offenders. Cut off as we are, it was difficult at first to find enough to occupy the men, for beyond a limited amount of geological work, seeing to the fabric of the hut and attending to the animals, etc., there was very little to be done in the way of serious work. I'm afraid a minority spent all too many hours writing letters and generally loafing. Since then, I've sent off two dog teams with further supplies for Corner Camp, instigated regular ski instruction, and organised seal-killing excursions.

At night some play cards, the rest read by the light of blubber lamps, a fuel-saving innovation thought up by Keohane and Birdie. We have a small collection of books which we interchange, with the exception of *A History of the Napoleonic Wars* belonging to Oates, which he appears never to get very far with. He told Bill he's been reading it for ten years.

For my part, I'm continually engaged in working on plans for the Polar journey, though they don't seem to be progressing as fast as I'd like. I'm conscious my mind is somewhat clouded at the moment. The thought of what *might* have happened to Bowers and Co. on the ice still haunts me. However, I've been thinking that when we get back to Cape Evans and settle in for the winter, it would be an excellent idea for the various scientific experts among us to give lectures on their special subjects – Simpson on coronas and auroras, Griffith-Taylor on modern physiography, Wright on ice formations, and so forth. In fact, we needn't confine ourselves to meteorological and geographical matters. For instance, Ponting could enlarge on photography, and Atkinson and Bill on parasites. Bill is absolutely marvellous when one gets him going on bloodsucking worms and the diseases they cause in man. We might even persuade Oates to give us his views on the management of horses.

When I told Bill of my idea, he was very enthusiastic. For the last few days he's been bullying everyone into a frenzy of sewing, patching and darning. I hadn't realised, until he pointed it out, how terribly negligent Englishmen can be in regard to the care of clothes. He says it's because they naturally shrink from looking as though they're playing the peacock. I suspect it has more to do with a reliance on women and servants.

Most mornings Bill and I march to Castle Rock to examine the state of the sea ice. It alternately melts and freezes. Our route back to Cape Evans lies over the worst corner of Erebus, and the whole mountainside appears to be a mass of crevasses. We might get over if we climbed to 4000 feet. We have long chats on these dawn excursions, mulling over things he realises I can't discuss in the hut. He understands me well enough to know that my continual harping on Amundsen's chances of beating us to the Pole isn't down to self-interest, or a longing for glory, simply a desire to reach, in an endless process of addition and subtraction,

116

a kind of mathematical peace. One hundred dogs, none of them presumably having fallen down a crevasse, must surely equal formidable odds.

It's ironic that the same situation should be happening to me all over again. It's barely three years since Shackleton sneaked off and nearly pipped me to the post. There again, I'd made no secret of my intentions. I'm not stupid enough to think of the Pole as mine, but I do detest underhandedness.

Sometimes Bill and I talk of personal matters, mostly on his initiative: mothers, fathers, wives. We don't go too deep. He says he misses his father. I counter by asserting I miss my mother, though I don't; I just hope the girls are looking after her and that she's not worrying about me.

'My father's such a steady man,' Bill says. 'I owe him everything.'

'My mother's been a brick,' I say. 'It's not been easy for her, what with my father gone, and Archie dying.'

It's true my mother was broken-hearted over my brother Archie's death, but my father's demise came as a merciful release – more so for her than him. He'd grown less careful in his later years, and my mother underwent humiliations.

'What sort of man was he?' asks Bill.

'The best,' I answer.

Bill says he misses Oriana. I admit to missing Kathleen. I haven't the faintest idea what *he* means by the word. I know what I mean, and missing seems a poor description for the amputation I'm suffering. Love is always selfish, and in my book all the better for it. Bill holds the opposite view, but then, being the puritan he is, he's more preoccupied with the spirit than the flesh, and I don't often get the feeling we're talking about the same thing.

Bill has made provision for Oriana, should things go

wrong. Her family has money too, so he has no worries on that score. I have nothing to leave Kathleen, because my first priority is my mother. She has been so wonderfully strong all these years, and I couldn't bear to think of her destitute.

Kathleen understands, and doesn't give a fig. She thinks I attach too much importance to material things. My mother was anxious when I said I was going to be married; she imagined Kathleen would object to my continuing to support her. It's a small enough amount, but it's still been a struggle to find it. I think, in time, my mother will come to realise what a splendid girl she has for a daughter-in-law. Why, when we were married I had to beg Kathleen to buy more suitable clothes. I was very much in the public eye, and it simply didn't do to have a wife dressed in Spanish shawls and black shrouds. I was alarmed at what she might wear at the altar, and asked my sisters to have a word with her; she sent them off with a flea in their ear. I needn't have worried. She looked like every other bride, only more radiant. She got her own back just before I slipped the ring on her finger by whispering that she thought the best man was very good-looking and she'd rather marry him.

Yesterday I told Bill I'd come to the conclusion there were three weak links in our party – four, if one counted Atkinson.

'What on earth has Atkinson done wrong?' he asked.

'That business of him going lame at Safety Camp,' I said.

'You can't blame a man for getting blisters,' he said.

It was the same when we got round to Meares and Gran. He said Gran was just a bit green round the ears and all he needed was a little support and encouragement.

'And what have you got against Meares?' he demanded. 'Apart from his wearing pyjamas on deck?'

'He's just not up to it,' I said. 'He's slack, and he made a terrible hash of purchasing the ponies.'

'Titus was supposed to go with him,' said Bill. 'At the last moment you agreed he should stay behind and help with the refitting of the ship.'

He was equally dogmatic when we discussed Teddy Evans. I'd known within three days of joining the *Terra Nova* at Port Chalmers that I'd made an error of judgment in appointing him my second in command, although my assessment wasn't proved until we set foot on land. Up until then he'd merely exhibited a kind of childishness, a lack of gravity, which I'd charitably put down to us all living hugger-mugger; some men need to feel the life and soul of the party. Which is why I renamed the *Skuary* after him. I thought it would buck him up. However, I've come to the belief he's not a rock to be built upon.

'Come now,' argued Bill, 'I grant you his continual high spirits can be a little irritating, but I wouldn't dismiss him out of hand. He gets on well with the men, and he's always anxious to help.'

'He may *want* to be helpful,' I said, 'but he's mentally incapable of being so. Though full of stout intentions, he simply lacks the intellectual ballast to make a significant contribution.'

'In the last resort,' countered Bill, 'physical rather than intellectual strength could be the saving of us.'

He had a point, albeit a disputable one. It's my belief the mind controls the body.

'He's also goodhearted,' said Bill. 'He doesn't bear grudges. Think of that business with Petty Officer Evans.'

'Good heavens,' I shouted, 'he practically ordered me to dismiss him. He can't stand Taff.'

'Very few of us can,' Bill said. 'Quite apart from the incident with Teddy's foot, no man likes to see his national flag draped over a tram terminus. And perhaps you've forgotten you *did* dismiss him, only to sign him on again.'

'It wasn't the national flag,' I said, lamely enough. 'It was the City of Cardiff flag.' I hadn't any real defence; Bill had right on his side. Taff had blotted his copybook in both Cardiff and New Zealand, and Teddy Evans had every cause for complaint. Nobody likes to have their boots pissed on, not by an inferior. And I *had* dismissed Taff, after he'd made a spectacle of himself falling overboard dead-drunk in Lyttelton; if Lashly hadn't dived in and fished him out, he might have perished. But then Taff, being the strenuous man he is, boarded my train to Port Chalmers and persuaded me to give him a second chance. 'Third,' I'd thundered, looking up at him in the doorway of the compartment. 'Cardiff seems to have slipped your mind.'

'That it hasn't, sir,' he lilted. 'Particularly the fund-raising dinner at the Royal Hotel, all them white lilies nodding in their vases, and Mrs Scott more beautiful than any of them.' After which bit of bunkum he launched into a rendering of the Welsh song which had roused so much patriotic, not to say financial, fervour in the stony breasts of the Chamber of Commerce.

Bill is the best friend I've ever had. While taking on board that I wrestle with imponderables – weights and measures, diet, altitudes, latitudes, climatic changes, animal capability, the evaluation of the men under my command – he still sees fit to keep me in check, defuse my anger and jolly me out of depression.

He's the only one I've told about my plans for the Polar journey. I see no reason to involve the others until I've got them quite fixed in my mind. We face a march of 400 miles across the Great Ice Barrier to the foot of the Beardmore Glacier. For this initial stage I intend to divide the party into three groups; a pony party of ten, two dog teams and a four-man motor party. Then twelve of us will climb 10,000 feet up the icy defile of the Queen Alexandra mountains to the Polar plateau where, split into three man-hauling sledge teams, we shall slog it south. The final assault will be made by four men. Bill altogether approves of these arrangements. How lost I should be without him.

A week later, I battled up Crater Hill. I was worried about the floe at Pram Point; besides, the longer I sit at the table, struggling with calculations, the more morose I become. Far better to keep on the move. The gusts were fierce and there was a heavy sea breaking over the ice foot. The spray carried right over the Point and rained on the roof of the hut. Vince's cross, thirty feet above the water, was continually battered. I don't ever remember such southerly winds.

Coming back, I saw several figures advancing on the hut. They turned out to be Griffith Taylor and party, returned from their geographical expedition to the Ferrar Glacier. At my approach Griff hesitated, not sure who I was. He said later he mistook me for a nigger. So much for Birdie's blubber contraptions.

By all accounts, Griff's trip has been highly worthwhile. Over supper he was forthright enough to declare they'd done more in six weeks than the *Discovery* scientists had accomplished in two years. He went further; he said previous findings were a disgrace. My stomach somersaulted once or twice, but I kept an interested smile on my face. Everyone had pulled their weight, Taff Evans in particular.

Later that night Taff asked if he could have a word. 'I hear very good reports of you,' I said.

'All in the line of duty, sir,' he replied, and stood there, shuffling his feet.

'Speak out,' I said. 'What is it?' I half thought he wanted to tell me the expedition had been a failure, that Griff had acted the Simon Legree.

'Well, sir,' he said, 'I missed my birthday. Leastways, we didn't have the opportunity, see, to mark the occasion. Now we're back, Clissold's going to bake me a cake.'

'A capital idea,' I said.

'Thing is,' he continued, 'it wouldn't be the same without you. I'd like you to be present, sir. If you could spare the time, sir.'

'Certainly,' I said. 'I wouldn't miss it for worlds.'

When I told Bill, he said I was showing favouritism. If I wasn't careful they'd all be asking me to attend their birthday celebrations. I knew there was no danger of that. Most of them would consider my presence a damper on the proceedings.

My regard for Taff Evans puzzles Bill. The most generous of fellows, he still can't quite understand what I see in the man, beyond the fact that we nearly died together falling down a crevasse. I imagine he thinks I'm flattered. I don't attempt to explain; the reasons are far too personal even for Bill to know. Nor am I blind to the obvious element of self-interest in Taff's regard for me.

The following day there was an unfortunate incident. I was standing outside the hut observing the skiing party through binoculars; Gran was supposed to be leading, but he was well behind, floundering on the slope. He looked back, and I swear he saw me and immediately clutched his leg and fell down. Some minutes later, emerging from a circle of concerned silhouettes, he began to limp hut-wards. I knew instantly what he was up to – at the very least he's an exhibitionist.

That morning I'd practically had to order him out of his bunk. He said he wasn't feeling too good. 'Report to Dr Atkinson,' I told him. Of course, he didn't. His attitude was openly slack. The way he dawdled over putting on his snow-shoes, his repeated yawning, alerted me to what might follow, which is why I'd been keeping an eye on him.

I didn't say anything when he came in. I waited two hours, until there were a fair number in the hut, and then, against Bill's earlier advice, denounced him as a malingerer. I knew what I was doing. He's 21 years of age, raw as an uncooked fish, and in his present state of mind as lethal as a killer whale. If I'm going to use him on the Polar journey, and I do need him, I can't allow him to behave as an individual. Such singular behaviour constitutes a danger. In the end it may well be every man for himself, but in the beginning it has to be every man for another. Should Gran fail to shoulder his share of the burden, none of us will survive.

He looked humiliated, which is understandable, and I daresay he'll hate the sight of me for some time to come, but he took it quite well, as I'd expected he would.

Afterwards, Bowers was kind enough to tell me he approved of what I'd done. I suspect the others had been muttering behind my back.

'It will stand him in good stead,' I said, and Bowers said, 'For a foreigner, he's not a bad cove. There's nothing wrong with him that a year in a good English public school wouldn't put to rights.' It was a pretty crass remark, but I pretended to go along with it.

Later, I overheard Oates telling Bill that Gran felt I was against him because of Amundsen. In due course Bill came to repeat what had been said, but I cut him short. 'I'm not interested in Oates's opinion,' I said. 'He makes no secret of the fact he's contemptuous of every other race save the British. I'm damned if I'm going to justify myself on his account, or yours, for that matter.'

This time I didn't bother to apologise to Bill. One grows sick of being thought in the wrong ...

*

The cutting of Taff's cake went off very well. I made a little speech along the lines of its being almost a decade since we met and how I valued knowing him. Clissold lit the candles, and we all sang 'Happy Birthday' – rather childish, really, when one thinks of our present position. As I expected, the men were relieved when I went back to my own part of the hut. I was just about to get down to my paperwork when Taff followed me.

'Well, Taff,' I said, 'that was all very pleasant.'

'I've been thinking, sir,' he blurted out, 'leastways, I gave it a lot of thought when me and Mr Griffith Taylor were on the glacier ... about my drinking, that is.'

'I'm sure that's all behind us now,' I said. 'You're hardly likely to be tempted here.'

'No,' he said. 'But I disgraced you, sir, and that saddens me.'

'Well,' I replied, 'we all make mistakes. I'd put it out of your mind.'

He still looked downcast, so I asked if there was

anything else that was troubling him.

'I didn't say good-bye properly to the Missus, sir. I wasn't as attentive as I might have been.'

'I know what you mean,' I said. 'It's hard to be as one would like.'

'I never kissed her goodbye, sir.'

'We all have our regrets,' I said.

When he'd gone I thought about Kathleen and that business of the photograph. Last year, long before the expedition got underway, she sent me a picture of her friend, the dancer Isadora Duncan, in one of her extravagant poses. I imagine Kathleen expected I'd be as enthusiastic over it as she was. I wasn't, and sent it straight back. If the truth be known, I found it absurd.

Kathleen has often lectured me on the necessity of my being shaken out of entrenched attitudes and of widening my horizons – before we sailed she said I had perhaps taken her too literally – and though I long to comply, if only to please her, I still think Miss Duncan something of a joke. But then Kathleen's background was very different from my own, and her family far from conventional. Mumbo's normal enough, but the same can't be said of their clergyman brother who often speaks from the pulpit with a barn owl perched on his shoulder. Once, in an extraordinary bid to raise money for his church, he drove round the parish with a walrus honking in the sidecar of his motor-cycle.

I wish now I hadn't sent back the photograph. It hurt her. I was hurt too; she did go on so about the qualities of grace, sensitivity and simplicity inherent in children, poets, fiddle-players, painters, factory-workers, hedge-cutters, dancers – everyone under God's sun save poverty-stricken naval lieutenants.

I was sitting there, lost in thought, when Bill pulled

up a chair and asked if I'd given any more consideration to his going off to Cape Crozier to the rookery of the Emperor penguin.

'No,' I told him, 'I can't say that I have. Though now you mention it, it occurs to me you might combine it with an experiment in diet, bearing in mind the Polar journey.'

'An excellent idea,' Bill said, looking eager.

'Perhaps each man could be put on a different proportion of fat to carbohydrates. What do you think?'

'An excellent idea,' he repeated, and added, 'It will be a terrific feather in the expedition's cap, you know, if we manage to pull it off.'

He was, of course, talking not of the Pole but of the Emperor penguin, a creature which cannot fly, lives on fish which it catches in the sea, never steps on land, not even to breed, and is the most primitive bird in existence. Unlike every other Antarctic bird which migrates north to breed, the Emperor goes south to a stretch of sea-ice so bleak that it's forced to use its own feet as a nest for its single egg; there's a little flap of skin hanging from the lower abdomen which serves as a covering. Ever since the *Discovery* days, when he'd seen chicks in September, Bill's been dreaming of bringing home a clutch of these eggs. According to him, a detailed examination of the embryos should provide the missing link between birds and reptiles.

'When would you be thinking of going?' I asked.

'Late June, early July,' he said. 'We should only be gone about ten days.'

'And who would you want along with you?'

'Bowers,' he answered promptly. 'And possibly young Cherry.'

'Good Lord, not Cherry,' I protested. 'Far better to

take Lashly or Crean.'

'No,' he said. 'I'd rather not take one of the men. They never look after their clothing, and besides, it's more fun travelling with one's own kind.'

Poor old Bill's never been at ease with men of a lower rank. It's not that he regards them as inferior, rather that he detests giving orders. I told him I couldn't give a definite answer, not right away. I promised I'd think about it, when I had less on my mind.

After he'd gone I thought about Kathleen again. I still don't know why she picked me from all her other admirers. She's always said she doesn't know either, beyond she wanted a son and 'knew' I should be his father. That, and what she refers to as my 'heavenly' eyes, which in moments of arousal apparently turn from blue to mauve. She told my mother, who was considerably taken aback, that she'd 'liked Con quite a lot' until Peter was born, and afterwards fallen violently in love. I'm only too thankful she didn't bring up the business of my eyes changing colour.

My love for her hasn't brought me contentment – how curious it is that passion has so little to do with feeling cheerful – but on occasions the intensity of our relationship has filled me with energy and gone some way towards obliterating the paralysing apathy which takes hold of me in times of stress or disappointment. If I'd met her when I was younger I would almost certainly have wished to die for her. Now I want to live.

I start to think of her a dozen times a day, and then stop myself, for that way madness lies – it sends me into daydreams in which I sail into port, the bands playing and the flags fluttering, happy ever after in never-never-land.

Lt. Henry Robertson (Birdie) Bowers
July 1911

Mid-winter night fell on June 22nd. We had an orgy, and no wonder, for on that date the sun began to turn back. I made a Christmas tree out of penguin feathers, split bamboo and ski sticks. Bill lay down on the ice and sang to the penguins, while I ran up and plucked at their backs. They were particularly immobilised by his rendering of 'For all the Saints that on this Earth do Dwell'. Though I say it myself, the resulting tree was a work of art.

Likewise the feast. We stuffed ourselves till we groaned – seal soup, roast beef and Yorkshire pudding, Brussels sprouts, anchovy pie, plum pudding flaming with brandy, crystallised fruits, champagne instead of our customary lime juice. Captain Scott was extremely gay during the meal and talked about his experiences as a torpedo lieutenant. Really, when he's in a relaxed mood there is absolutely no one more charming or likeable in the whole world, and that includes Uncle Bill. He positively lights up one's heart.

Outside the hut, as if in celebratory accord, the heavens put on their celestial crown, and all night long the aurora flashed its golden beams above the smoking crater of Mount Erebus. When I went out to take the meteorological readings, the snow rang to the thud of my footsteps. Beyond the Point the ice cracked as the temperature fell and the water rose.

We all got presents, bought in mid-summer a year ago by mothers, sisters, wives, and long kept hidden in a special box marked 'festivities'. None of the gifts came labelled; we just dipped in, and there was nothing showy or expensive amongst them. Titus Oates received a whistle, a pop-gun and a sponge, all of which pleased him no end.

I expect the gun came from Mrs Scott, whom I won't forget waltzing with in New Zealand. It's all right a chap looking at one fair and square, but it's damned disconcerting coming from a woman. She knew she'd got me pinned down, because she kept smiling. 'Lt. Bowers,' she said, 'I assure you I won't eat you.' I didn't altogether believe her, yet I admired her tremendously, and later was relieved to notice she looked at inaminate objects – lampshades, vases of flowers – with much the same intensity of gaze. My parcel included a ball of wool and some knitting needles, but I imagine these came from one of my sisters.

Ponting gave a lecture, with slides, of the photographs he's taken since we arrived; the shore party landing stores, preparing for the depot journey, Osman with his head on Meares's lap, all of us round the table at the old *Discovery* hut, faces black with blubber smoke; lastly, an absolutely ripping study of the *Terra Nova* anchored in McMurdo Sound, the ice waves bunched like burst pillows in the foreground.

His commentary was somewhat flowery. 'Here we see the assiduous Dr Wilson in the process of making an artistic sketch of the distant view of the fairy slopes of the western mountains ... here we observe Captain Scott, our gallant leader, overseeing the landing of the

130

motorised transport.' It didn't help that he'd captured
the Owner, mouth open in dismay, leaping back in
shock as the biggest motor plunged through the ice and
sank to the bottom of the Sound.

I'm afraid none of us were in a condition to be
appreciative. I took it we were all embarrassed at seeing
ourselves through the lens of the camera. I know I was.
I can't fathom why everyone says my headgear makes
me look like a pirate; to my eyes I resemble my mother
in her gardening hat.

When the table was cleared we attempted to play
Snapdragon, but such was the unholy din going on
around us, what with the gramophone constantly being
rewound, and Teddy Evans and Griff bawling out,
'Blow, bullies blow, For Californ-i-o', each verse
growing more bawdy than the last, each chorus
accompanied by a flurry of blows to the biceps, that we
soon gave up.

Some time in the small hours Titus danced the
Lancers with Anton, the Russian groom, who put up a
wonderful performance, flinging his legs about like a
man possessed by demons. Originally, he was only hired
by Meares to look after the ponies as far as New
Zealand, but he proved such a stalwart little worker, the
Owner kept him on. Poor Anton, he didn't know what
he was in for. Uneducated as he is, he's taken the
darkness badly. Not having a grasp of the turning of the
earth, he has a superstitious fear the sun has gone
doolally for ever. Convinced that the phosphorescent
lights which leap up from the sea are evil spirits, he
chucked his precious ration of cigarettes into the water
to appease them. Oates caught him in the act. His
belongings are ready-packed under his bunk for the
return of the *Terra Nova*. All he wants to do, or so he

told Titus, is to get back home and marry his one-legged sweetheart.

After this display, Titus went round asking whether any of us were sweating. If we said no, he promptly dabbed our faces with his sponge, now dipped in gravy, and shouted, 'Well, you are now … by Jove you are!' Then he rushed about shooting everybody with his pop-gun. We'd toasted the returning sun in milk, but I expect he'd mixed his with something more fiery. Finally, he aimed his gun at Captain Scott and asked, 'How doth Homer have it? I blew it into the cerulean azure.' To which Captain Scott replied, 'You're a good fellow, Titus. Why not call it a day?'

This was a hint for the company to retire pretty sharpish, and we did, all except Titus who slouched off to the stables, where at intervals he could be heard blowing blasts on his whistle.

Meares, who's a great traveller, began to whisper us a bloodcurdling story about the Chinese and their war with the Lolas, one of the eighteen tribes on the borders of Tibet. The Chinese took a Lolo hostage, tied him to a bamboo bench, slit his throat and dipped their flag into his blood. Then they cut out the poor devil's heart and liver and cooked them for supper.

'What rag?' asked Gran, and for some reason this made us burst with laughter, or rather we stuffed our faces into our mattresses to drown the roars we made.

Some time after, Titus returned, shook Cherry awake and asked him if he was responsible for his actions, and Cherry called out plaintively, 'Go away, you shan't have my liver!' which set us all off again.

I was just drifting into sleep when Titus tumbled Meares out of his bunk and demanded to know if he was fancy-free. Meares punched him. I was astonished the

Owner, a very moderate drinker, didn't rise up and give them both a roasting.

Five days later, Bill, Cherry and I prepared to leave for the penguin rookery at Cape Crozier. We had two sledges, one tied behind the other, both heaped high with camping equipment, provisions, pick-axes, ropes, repair kits, hurricane lamps, medical supplies, etc., also a case full of scientific gear for pickling and preserving. Their combined weight was enormous – 757 lbs.

I never thought the Owner would let us go, not with the Polar trek only three months off, but somehow Bill managed to talk him round. To reach the rookery, where temperatures often register 100 degrees of frost, it's necessary to scramble down cliffs exposed to blizzards sweeping ferociously across hundreds of miles of open snow plain. And all this in the dark! Exciting stuff, what?

Since our return to Cape Evans I've been putting my fourpence in with the best of them, and I rather imagine the Captain wanted to give me a treat after the appalling events of the breaking up of the sea-ice. At any rate, he raised no objections as far as I was concerned, though he balked at the idea of Cherry floundering about the Crozier cliffs in the depths of winter. I suspect he was thinking of the fate of seaman Vince. He gave in eventually – Bill badgered him so.

Cherry's terribly bucked at being included. He's down on the list as assistant zoologist to Uncle Bill, and has come in for a fair amount of ragging, seeing all he studied was the classics. 'We're well aware of your qualifications for Antarctic exploration,' Teddy Evans told him in an unguarded moment during the mid-winter feast. 'A thousand pounds and an ability to read Latin and Greek.'

We were standing there adjusting the loads when Captain Scott approached, frowning heavily. 'Bill, why are you taking all this oil?' he asked, looking at the six tins lashed to the second sledge. Bill muttered something to the effect that it was better to be safe than sorry and that we'd be bringing most of it back, but one could tell the Owner was annoyed. He's understandably loth to squander provisions on anything other than the southern journey. All the same, as Bill later remarked, we could hardly be expected to embark on such a mission carrying nothing more substantial than a tin of Huntley and Palmer biscuits and a blubber-streaked copy of *Bleak House*.

I think I know what ails the Owner. He's absolutely sound as regards what's right, but he lacks conviction. He simply isn't stupid enough to be convinced his is the only way. In the circumstances, it's a dangerous trait.

There was a seal-killing party setting out at the same time, the Owner parading up and down to make sure things were ship-shape. He himself rarely accompanies these forays, and when he does I've noticed he's apt to look in the opposite direction during the actual butchering. I'd thought it was because he couldn't stand the sight of blood, but Bill says it's the slaughter that turns his stomach. I must admit it's a messy business; one has to club them on the nose before sticking a knife in their hearts, and they have extraordinarily expressive eyes. I can't help remembering the Temple of the Tooth in Ceylon with its pictures depicting the Buddhist hell. One could only thank God they were fanciful, as most of them went beyond description for fiendish ingenuity, the worst torments being reserved for the killers of animals. In comparison, Dante's *Inferno* would seem like a pleasure garden.

A few of the fellows came up to wish us godspeed, all of them wearing expressions pitched between mirth and pity. I don't doubt they believed us mad as hatters. Bill and I didn't care. I've been five times round the world, and Bill quite as far in his mind, yet we still thought this an awfully big adventure. I'm not so sure about Cherry, but then, he generally looks as though he expects somebody to go for him with the boxing gloves.

At the last moment Ponting wanted to take our photograph. Reluctantly we lined up – Bill with his hand on his hips, Cherry smiling bashfully, myself leaning on a ski-stick. Caught in the flashlight we froze, three men about to go bird's-nesting.

*

Cape Crozier is sixty-seven miles from Cape Evans, and within two days we covered the fifteen miles to Hut Point. It was to be the last time we achieved such distances on our marches. As early as the first day I think both Bill and I began to realise what we'd let ourselves in for. He didn't smile again, not wholeheartedly. Though his mouth crinkled up, his eyes remained worried.

On the depot-laying journey we'd got into a rhythm of marching, and when we camped we did so as a team, each man having routine duties to perform. While some unlashed the sleeping bags, others put up the tents, fetched snow for water, had the primuses assembled, the food bags undone and so on. But now there were only three of us, and the loads were terribly heavy, and none of us had ever been out in such degrees of cold. Other people had travelled to Cape Crozier before us, including Bill, but never in winter, never in darkness.

Strain as we might we could never get up enough speed to stop our feet from going numb, for the snow clung to the runners in powdered clumps and acted like brakes, and we were forever stopping to scrape them clear. We couldn't see where we were going, where we were stepping, where the food bags were, or the straps for the sledges, couldn't read the compass without using three or four boxes to strike one dry match. And when we did find what we wanted, the cords and the straps and the lashings had frozen to the hardness of wire which had to be undone and retied through three thicknesses of gloves. Cherry was foolish enough that first day to bare his hands to unbuckle his harness, and instantly Jack Frost bit all ten of his fingers. The next morning the fluid in the blisters had turned to ice. We were lucky in that the Owner had decided we should conduct a dietary experiment, for this cut down on the amount of bags we had to open, and we carried only pemmican, tea, biscuits and butter. It would be interesting to determine, he had speculated, as we'd sat of an evening round the stove, whether such restricted fare would provide all the fat, proteids and carbo-hydrates needed for man-hauling in extreme conditions.

We panted like dogs when pulling the loads, and heard our breath crackle as it solidified on the air. We sweated from the effort, and that froze too. If we were quick enough, or had heart enough, we could jump up and down and shake the particles out above our boots, but mostly it sank into the material of our clothing and suited us in armour. Unless I kept my face turned away from the notebook in which I jotted down meteorological readings, a film of ice formed on the paper and rendered my pencil useless. We took hours to make camp and hours to break camp, and in between tottered like children across the immensity of that bleak and hiemal playground.

Quite soon – I think we were approaching the desolate bay that lies between Hut Peninsula and Terror Point – we found we couldn't shift both sledges together. When the temperature on the Barrier surface reaches a certain low point the runners can't melt the crystals, and one can only advance by rolling them over and upon one other. I suppose it's a bit like ploughing. We were forced to relay, which meant that for every three painful miles we covered we only went one mile forward. That first night there was no wind and we trudged back by candlelight and Jupiter.

It was a measure of Bill's flexibility that he quickly abandoned the notion of night and day, for in truth there was nothing to mark the difference. The cold never lessened, and apart from an hour at what passed for midday, when a dim and ghostly twilight stained the horizon, the blackness was absolute. Often we went without lunch because it was simply too painful to go through that whole wretched rigmarole of unpacking and repacking. We marched until we could go no further, or until Bill imagined Cherry's feet were in danger. He never gave a thought to his own. The onset of frostbite is interesting, in that the warning symptoms, mainly a tingling of the affected parts, are similar to those of the thawing-out process.

We made no attempt to attend to our frozen extremities until we'd eaten. The effect of hot food was nothing short of miraculous, as though it by-passed the usual channels of ingestion and entered straight into the bloodstream. As Bill rightly said, it was like putting a hot-water bottle to one's heart. Then, it was easier to unwind our puttees, lever off our frozen finneskö and socks and begin to nurse our feet back to feeling.

We even managed to laugh at the spectacle we made, Cherry leaning back with his toes paddling for warmth beneath Bill's wind jacket and undervest, Bill doubled forward, his hands tucked into Cherry's armpits, me with my nose held over the pan steaming on the cooker. If Ponting had been with us he'd have had a field day with his camera, though Lord knows what others would have construed from the images.

I don't understand by what magic I've been spared, but I was undoubtedly less affected by the cold than either Bill or Cherry. Never once since we made landfall have my feet become frozen. Oates, Meares, Atkinson, the Owner, even Gran, they've all been caught pretty badly at one time or another. Perhaps it has something to do with my height, or rather the lack of it, in that being closer to the ground my blood has less far to circulate. Whatever the reason, I can stand low temperatures better than the other fellows, a fact Bill finds strange, seeing I've spent most of my life in the tropics. It's only my nose that ever gets nipped, it being so damnably prominent.

That isn't to say I got away entirely scot-free, for I had fearsome stomach cramps from our diet. Bill was on extra fat, Cherry had been persuaded to go for carbohydrates – he was usually doubled up with heartburn – and I was experimenting with proteids. I found I couldn't eat all my pemmican ration, Bill balked at his quantity of butter, while Cherry complained of hunger and a craving for sweet things. He said he had a picture sitting in his head of a tin of peaches in thick syrup. In my opinion, the Huntley and Palmer biscuits made up from a secret recipe of Bill's in consultation with a chemist, provided all the sugar we needed. There were two sorts, one called 'Antarctic', and the other 'Emergency', but as either label seemed to furnish a correct description of the pickle we were in, we ate both and never noticed the difference. I thought a lot about wedges of freshly baked bread, and boiled potatoes sprinkled with salt.

On the sixth night – we were now into July and that day had slogged ten miles to gain three – Bill suggested we turn back.

'Rather not,' said Cherry. He was crouching over the cooker, pricking his blisters with a knife and blissfully wincing.

'What do you think, Birdie?' asked Bill. I knew he was wanting advice rather than an heroic, gung-ho affirmative.

'Well,' I said, 'there's no denying conditions are far worse than we could have imagined, and I expect they'll get worse.'

'Dear God,' he interjected.

'But,' I continued, 'we have sufficient food, are in pretty rude health, and it strikes me that collecting these eggs is a jolly worthy enterprise. I happen to believe we can stick it.'

I was speaking no more than the truth, having always found that willpower overcomes all adversities. One just has to believe that it's within one's spiritual domain to conquer difficulties. That is not to say that I don't recognise there has to be a time to submit, possibly a time to die, merely that I've never yet been taken to the brink.

Aware of this lack of experience, I added, 'It's your decision, Uncle Bill, but speaking for myself, I say we go on.' At which Cherry nodded vigorously.

Bill cheered up after this and waxed on about the penguins. I must say they lead terrible lives, in that their undoubted maternal instinct leads more to infanticide than nurturing.

'In their desire to further the existence of the species,' Bill informed us, 'they often trample their young to death. It's a matter of too many mothers in charge of too few eggs.'

'Smothering love,' exclaimed Cherry.

'If one of them should leave their egg unattended for a moment,' Bill said, 'another rushes up and instantly makes off with it, with the result they often get broken. The bereft bird sometimes goes to the lengths of fashioning an egg out of a lump of ice ... it's quite pathetic to watch the way they carry it around in the expectation of it hatching.'

He and Cherry usually went on talking for an hour or more, by which time I was in the land of dreams. We were all troubled by nightmares on the winter journey, but whereas I drifted back into sleep Bill and Cherry apparently tossed and turned until the shivering dawn. Bill was hounded awake by images of that silver bird he'd glimpsed from the crow's nest of the *Terra Nova*, and dear old Cherry was chased by a flood of treacle which threatened to engulf him. I could never remember what visions disturbed me. Bill used to say it gave him immense pleasure to lie there listening to my oblivious snores.

That first, awful week we thought conditions had got about as bad as we could possibly encounter, and we were wrong. After rounding Cape Mackay we ran into a series of blizzards of such icy ferocity that our minds threatened to become as numbed as our bodies. We were almost worse off in the tent than out of it, for our breath and the steam from the cooker deposited a rim of hoar frost on the inner lining which, if we left the cooker burning long enough, gradually melted and dripped mercilessly down upon us. Our sleeping bags were daily turned into frozen boards, and in trying to prise them open one had to be careful lest the leather broke like glass. And then, of course, once they had thawed sufficiently for us to force our way into them, it was like lying in a damp ditch until, the cooker extinguished and the temperature plummeting, the outer covering began to stiffen all over again.

I don't know why I found it so easy to sleep, but I did; sometimes, or so the others told me, I dozed off in the middle of a conversation. During those moments when I was dragged back to consciousness by the agony of stomach cramps, I felt Cherry shuddering against my back. One night, dreaming I was watching a tap dancer on the stage of the music-hall, his arms hung forward in that peculiar puppet stance, I woke to hear the chattering of Bill's teeth.

Blizzard-bound, we passed the time speculating on who might be in that final party to reach the Pole. Both Cherry and I thought Bill would be one of them, for old time's sake, but he insisted he was a scientist not a foot slogger, and he guessed the Owner would probably take myself and the two seamen, Lashly and Crean. I said surely Oates would be picked instead of me, and what about Teddy Evans, at which Bill laughed and said Evans hadn't one chance in a hundred of being included. When we'd exhausted the possibilities, we conjectured what Amundsen was up to, and whether his chances were better than our own, bearing in mind the number of dogs he had with him.

Bill was cautious; I suspect he knew a lot more about

the Owner's plans than he let on. 'There's no doubt,' he said, 'that dogs have always been considered preferable to other forms of transport, but we haven't really tested the efficiency of the motor vehicles.'

'Lashly says they only work on perfectly flat surface,' Cherry argued. 'And only in certain temperatures.'

'In my opinion,' I told them, 'I think there's an unsporting element in the use of either motors or dogs. Far better to stride out, nation against nation, man against man.'

Bill held I was perhaps clinging to the inappropriate chivalry of a bygone age.

'I see no reason to be ashamed of that,' I retorted.

'Then you see eye to eye with Con,' Bill said, in a tone of voice which coming from him was positively chilling. 'I just hope the rest of us don't have cause to regret such romantic notions.'

Somewhat taken aback, I dropped the subject and switched to a topic we never tired of, namely what we might do when the whole exciting business was over and done with and we were back in England. 'I shall spend an entire week swimming,' I vowed. 'And before that, an entire week eating.'

Bill said he intended to make straight for the woods near Crippets, his childhood home in the vicinity of Cheltenham. 'I got more joy from those woods,' he lamented, 'and learnt more of things worth knowing than anywhere else on earth. It's the haunt of the badger, the fox and the owl, and in spring the bluebells mirror the colour of the sky.'

'Don't,' said Cherry, looking fit to cry.

'When I had tuberculosis I used to go there at dawn, light my pipe, lean against a tree stump clutching *Modern Painters* and the New Testament, and watch the first sunbeams gradually lighting up the corners of the glade. I've never known such happiness. Of course, I believed I was dying, which alone brings extraordinary peace of mind.'

This rather silenced Cherry. Pressed, he astonished Bill and me by blurting forth his ambition of taking out to supper every girl he met. 'She wouldn't even have to be pretty,' he stuttered. 'Just so long as she seemed to like me.'

The blizzards subsiding, we stumbled onwards. Being the shortest, I led on the traces, Cherry and Bill fanning out behind. In the darkness Cherry was doubly blind; he could never wear his spectacles on the marches.

A curious thing happened when we were relaying the sledges. With only the candle to light the way we found it easier to tread back in our earlier footprints, and at first there was nothing remarkable in our progress. Then I became aware that both Bill and Cherry were floundering behind more than usual. On looking round I was astonished to see they were advancing as though prancing over hot coals. Apparently their footsteps, due to some optical delusion, appeared before them as elevations rather than depressions, and they found themselves compelled to raise their feet to step over what they took to be hummocks. I wasn't affected. They called each other all kinds of a fool, but it didn't help, and they were forced into the absurdity of continuing to clamber over phantom mounds. If it hadn't been so wearisome we might have laughed.

On the twelfth day the temperature registered -69 degrees. Cherry crawled out of the tent and turned his head to the right, and instantly his balaclava froze to his wind-jacket. For four hours he had to pull with his head stuck in that position. Our clothing, with its accumulation of ice, was now becoming as heavy as lead, as were our sleeping-bags, and in the comparative warmth of the tent we lay in sodden misery. The days' marches compared to the night 'rests' were heavenly, and both intervals of time were terrible beyond belief. Strange to think that in my mother's garden the gold light of summer danced upon the maple leaves. Every morning, after I'd fumbled through the hour or more it took to light the candle in the lantern, Bill asked, 'Should we turn back?' and the answer mumbled through cracked lips was always the same, 'No, we'll stick it out.'

I don't know what kept the others going, beyond the fact that Bill wanted his penguin embryos and Cherry was prepared to follow him to hell if need be. For my part, I felt there was something splendid, sublime even, in pitting oneself against the odds. I've always been fortunate in the things I've wanted to do, always achieved the goals I've set myself. Over the years I've bumped into fellows I was on the *Worcester* with, and quite a few of them, not having got anywhere quick enough, had given up the sea and were sitting behind desks in dusty offices, and others of the same age as myself were still no further forward than first mate of some leaky barque trading between Australia and the Philippines.

There is a portion of my life, of course, which has been less satisfactory. I'm well aware of how physically unprepossessing I must appear to the opposite sex, yet none the less I dream of meeting a girl who could care for me, the sort of girl my father found in my beloved mother. Those sisters I met in Melbourne, Dorothy and Mary, were frightfully nice. I liked Dorothy best, but she was the prettiest and had all the fellows flocking round her, and I'm just no good at dancing and paying

compliments and all that rot. I never discovered which
one sent me the jam, but I hope it was Dorothy. Seeing I
haven't yet reached thirty, I comfort myself with the
thought there must be someone out there waiting for
me to come through a door. And in the meantime, life is
great fun and I couldn't be more contented with my lot.
The world is changing, and soon the machine will be of
more importance than the body, and it's tremendous
luck to have been born into the last few seconds of an
epoch in which a man is still required to stand up and be
counted.

It took us nineteen days to reach Cape Crozier. Bill
was terribly bothered, as he'd told the Owner we'd be
there and back in ten. I think I knew by then we'd get
through. Sometime in the second week, when we were
floundering across the pressure ridges, Mt Terror
above us, but invisible, and the Barrier to our right, the
moon flitted out from behind the clouds, and there,
only five paces ahead of us, was a gigantic crevasse
lidded with a shiny covering of thin ice. At the time we
were running downhill, the sledges at our heels and, but
for that sudden pale illumination we would most
certainly have perished. I understood then that
providence was on our side; it was unthinkable to
believe God would save us simply to prolong the agony.

From then on Bill insisted on going ahead with the
lantern to make sure the surface was firm. I wanted to
take my turn but he begged me to do as he bade. 'I got
us into this mess,' he said, 'and I simply couldn't bear it
if anything happened to you and Cherry.'

It wasn't all misery. On one of our halts we lay
spread-eagled on the ice and stared up at a sky blazing
with the glory of the most wonderful aurora I'd ever
witnessed. I groaned beneath the splendour of those

silken curtains, yellow, green, and orange, billowing at the window of the heavens.

'Tell me, tell me,' pleaded Cherry; without his glasses the whirling display was but a blur.

I don't know what I told him, for the effects were at first mesmeric, then hallucinatory. I was falling, diving towards a sea whose ripples spread and widened until they touched the edges of my soul. I know at one point Bill began to squeal with laughter – our lips were so split and caked with dried blood it was painful to open them fully – and when we demanded to know what was funny, he said, 'Ask me what I'm doing here, you dear fellows.'

Ever obliging, Cherry croaked, 'What are you doing here, Uncle Bill?' And he replied, 'I've never liked crowds', and then we all squealed, because we could see the humour of it: three ragged, frosted figures lying on their backs in the darkness of nowhere, emitting cries like stuck pigs as God's own paintbrush splashed among the stars.

At last we reached the Cape, and in a snowy dip between the twin peaks of the Knoll, 800 feet above the sea, we pitched our last camp and set to work to build the igloo. This was Bill's pet project; before we left we spent hours poring over the sketches he made of this temporary refuge of ice and stones. He called it Oriana's house, and sometimes we'd pretended to squabble as to where the sofa and the bookcases would go and who should have the bedroom overlooking the sea.

We'd even practised building one like it on the shore below the hut, but that was in daylight and in the 'mildness' of March, and here the ice had hardened to the consistency of marble, and it was fearful labour

146

cutting the blocks for the walls and shovelling the bits of gravel and drifted snow with which to pack the cracks. Still, in two days it was finished, the canvas roof secured, the blubber stove in place, and then we fought our way into those devilish sleeping-bags, whereupon I, at least, slept the sleep of the dead.

We rose at three the next morning, into moonlight misty with fog. It's at Cape Evans that the Barrier, that great wall of ice which extends 400 miles south and east, meets the land, and we could just make out the tumultuous shapes of the pressure fields jostling the smudged edge of the frozen sea. On Bill's reckoning it was four miles to the cliffs, and he wanted to get there by midday so as to have the benefit of the twilight hour. Blubber for the stove was now a more urgent priority than Emperor eggs; we were a quarter of a way through the fifth of those six precious tins of oil the Owner had so begrudged our taking.

The last two miles took us through the pressure ridges, and by then the moon had gone. Imagine an acre, newly ploughed, in the heart of the English countryside, the noonday sun filtering through the branches of the oak trees at the boundary, the plump plough-horses standing motionless in the shade, the ploughboy fast asleep with his hat over his eyes. Then imagine, if you can, a field churned up by the flails of a plough so monstrous in size that the ensuing furrows sink sixty feet, the embankments on either side twisted and fissured into tortured mounds of glittering ice veined with crevasses, the whole landscape dim as the interior of a cave in which every shadow fades to deepest black. If you can imagine this, you may still have only the faintest, foggiest grasp of what we were up against.

When we did get through, roped together and working with pickaxes, Bill couldn't find his old route between the rock wall and the ice cliff. No matter how many attempts we made to clamber downwards, there was always too huge an obstacle or too great a drop. Then Bill would veer in another direction and shout out a warning of a crevasse ahead. I would cross, followed by Cherry, who, all but blind without his spectacles, stepped time without number into the void. Poor fellow, he was dreadfully upset at being such a handicap to us.

'I'm so sorry,' he panted, on each occasion we hauled him out. 'I should never have come.'

'You're the best travelling companion a chap could wish for,' I assured him. 'Even if you do keep giving us the slip.'

'It's not your fault,' Bill told him. 'If anyone's to blame, I am', and he gripped Cherry's arm and begged him to be careful.

On we blundered, staggering, rolling down snow-slopes, the sledge catching our heels and knocking us off our feet. We were like flies fluttering against a window that would never open. And by now the twilight had faded. At last, exhausted, we floundered to a halt, all but sinking to our knees. It was then, from somewhere below us on the sea-ice, we heard the Emperors calling.

I can't tell you how bucked we were, especially for Bill. I was all for going on, but he said it was far too dangerous and we needed food and rest. On the way back I don't think any of us gave much thought to the crevasses; we were past caring and it was time to put our trust in Someone else, for we had gone beyond the point when we could look after ourselves.

I swear my mother was with me, or rather waiting

somewhere ahead, not smiling or beckoning, but there all the same, the firelight flickering across her dear face, her Moody and Sanky hymn book on her lap. There was a moment, levering Cherry up from yet another crevasse, when I thought I heard her singing, and I turned my head to one side the better to catch the tune. I'm not ashamed to say tears came into my eyes, of affection not weakness, tears which froze as they fell.

That night we camped in Oriana's house and used up yet more oil cooking our supper. We'd gone without food two nights running to save on fuel, making do with a drink of hot water, and I think Cherry might have died if we'd done so again. Truth to tell, the tent with its double lining was warmer than the igloo, but we'd shifted the cooker and the sleeping bags and were simply too done in to lug them back again.

Bill was fearfully alarmed at the state of our clothing. Once they were half-way thawed we'd got into the habit of wrapping them round our limbs in order to prevent them sticking out at odd angles, but it was a risky business; sometimes they froze so tightly to our bodies it was like being encased in armour, with the result we could hardly drag one leg after the other. My green hat, which I'd adapted for the journey by adding ear flaps and neck guards and whatnot, was a never-failing source of amusement. If I'd fallen asleep with it still in place I woke to find its appendages hanging about my cheeks, and when I went outside and pushed them out of the way they froze into the most astonishing shapes. Often I marched with what appeared to be a jerry balanced on my head, handles and all, and another time, ducking my way out of the tent after one of the blizzards, a shower of drift settled on the top and instantly sculptured itself into a rough approximation of an alighting bird, though God knows, an ornithologist would have been hard put to name the species. Spying it, Cherry sang out: 'For you don't know Nellie like I do/Said the naughty little bird on Nellie's hat', which was the chorus of one of Meares's favourite gramophone records back at Cape Evans.

We got up early again, and it was no great hardship. I can't pretend we were rested, yet we were cheerful enough, the experiences of the day before having convinced us that the pressure ridges ran further out into the bay than in *Discovery* times, and that Bill's old route had gone. We'd made up our minds there was only one way down – over the cliffs. A 200-foot descent in darkness was unthinkable, but I'd spotted a break in the rocks from which hung an ice-floe. It was just possible we could get down to the rookery on this.

We reached the cliffs seven hours later and descended a fair distance, cutting steps where our crampons couldn't find a foothold, scrambling over and under those gigantic growths squeezed up by the moving ice, only to meet a glacial wall which even a madman would have recognised as impassable. Like spiders we crawled sideways, and suddenly Bill shouted out triumphantly, 'Birdie, over here!', and there in front of us was a black tunnel burrowed into the ice, just wide enough for a man to enter.

'Here goes,' Bill said, and we followed him, wriggling and slithering through that fox's hole until we emerged on a crystallised ledge above the bay. Below us, uttering metallic cries of alarm and looking like so many overworked waiters, strutted the Emperor penguins.

There was a snorter of a drop onto the sea-ice, not so difficult to make if one was planning on staying below, but ticklish if one was contemplating coming up again.

Cherry volunteered to stay behind to haul us aloft; being blind as a bat, this was no more than sensible.

Bill and I slaughtered three of the Emperors for their blubber – each bird weighed in excess of six stone – and took five of their eggs. Bill was concerned at the decline in their numbers. The *Discovery* expedition had found over 2000 birds breeding in the bay, and now there were less than a hundred, and half of those were without eggs. I thought them peculiarly and disturbingly human, in that when we lunged forward to plunge a knife into their breasts, and missed, they waddled further off and then stopped to look back, standing there in an attitude of saintly reproachfulness. I couldn't decide whether they were stupid or possessed of superior intelligence, and prayed it was the former.

Getting back up the cliff was a nightmare. The rope got snagged and we dangled round and round, fighting for a foothold on that slippery incline. Not once throughout our dreadful journey had a cross word come between us, nor had we forgotten the civilities, those please-and-thank-yous which can mean so much when everything else has gone by the board. When it came to it, none of us had dodged the column and each had put the other's welfare above his own. I believe Bill and Cherry to be giants among men, incapable of self-interest, and time and again I saw them snap their fingers in the face of the Prince of Darkness – and now, when the rope was slack and Cherry's pickaxe came hurtling past us, Bill broke and shouted out, 'Cherry, for God's sake, man, pull.'

As it happened, I don't think Cherry took it amiss. He was half delirious with exhaustion, his frost-bitten fingers bulging like plums. When Bill reached the top and apologised for his outburst, gripping Cherry's

gloves in his own, Cherry all but fainted at the pressure.
'My fault,' he gasped, as though he was a papist. 'My
most grievous fault.'

We took the five eggs back in our mitts. Both of
Cherry's smashed on the way, for he fell so often.
Earlier, the wind had got up, and now it grew worse,
covering our tracks. Before long it was blowing force
four and we floundered about, first in one direction,
then another, sometimes doubling backwards in an
effort to find the igloo. Cirrus cloud whirled across the
north stars and there was a haze of fog to the south.

I've read stories in which weary travellers, lost in the
mists on some rugged moor, come at last to a
comfortable inn at the wayside, the landlord waiting
with hot grog, the fire roaring in the hearth, clean
sheets spread across goose feather mattresses. Our
particular inn, when we did finally stumble across it, let
in the wind and the snowdrift, yet we thought it the
most hospitable place on earth.

It took two hours to get the blubber stove lit; just as it
began to burn more strongly a blob of boiling fat spat
into Bill's eye. He reckoned his sight had gone and
thrust his arm against his mouth to stifle his groans. It
was well-nigh unbearable not being able to do anything
for him beyond uttering platitudes and watching him
suffer.

Cherry was a tower of strength. Going outside, he
plugged up as many of the gaps in the walls as he could
find. His fingers were now easier, he said, and he put it
down to the oil in the broken eggs in his mitts.

When we'd eaten and were a little warmer we
discussed our situation. I was all for making another
descent to the rookery, yet I knew it was out of the
question – Cherry and Bill were almost at the end of

their tether, we had one tin of oil left for the return journey, and our clothing was in rags. Bill said we ought to rest up, wait for calmer weather and then make a run for home. 'We've reached rock-bottom,' he said faintly, pressing a wad of cotton rag dunked in cold tea to his injured eye. 'Things must improve.'

That night I dreamt I was on that other ghastly run, the St Paul's Journeys, an initiation torture devised for new cadets on the *Worcester*. The victim had to sprint the length of the lower deck and back, and then to his hammock under the top hammocks of the older chaps who hit him with boots, rope, knotted towels, anything that hurt. I could hear my heart thumping in my chest as I ran and the shouts of those bully-boys above me. All my youthful enthusiasm and ideals had melted away, replaced by cunning and an animal necessity to go to ground. Then it became very quiet – the other fellows vanished, and there was nobody but me standing there, eyes wide with terror. A sob burst from me – or so I thought. I woke instantly, to a terrible suffocating silence. The next moment I heard a second, greater sob, a fearsome gulp of sound fit to swallow the universe.

Scrambling out of my bag I opened the igloo door, at which the world suddenly cracked wide open, the wind shrieking about my ears, a solid wall of black snow crushing me to my knees. As if under water I dog-paddled those few yards to the tent, came up against the provision boxes, felt for that neat row of finneskö, that canvas sack containing a copy of *Bleak House* and the poems of Tennyson, the tin of sweets I'd brought to celebrate Bill's birthday. I crawled back, calling for Cherry, and twice I was flung on my face by the force of the wind. 'The tent's gone,' I shouted.

Cherry and I laboured for what seemed like years

transferring the gear to the igloo. All but crazy from the pain of his eye, Bill could do no more than lie in the doorway and blindly shovel the drift from the entrance.

I don't know what the other two were thinking while we sank into hell. I know there were two halves of me, one which raced ahead working out ways of getting back to Cape Evans by means of digging holes in the ice and using the ground sheet as a covering, and the other which longed to curl up in the igloo and acknowledge we were done for.

It wasn't that I'd given up hope, rather that the loss of the tent and the inhuman fury of the hurricane tearing at the canvas roof, so that it rattled as though we were under continuous rifle-fire, had the same hallucinatory effect as the auroral display of our outward journey and drove me into dreams. I relived the moment when I opened the igloo door and heard that mighty crack of the elements, and sometimes I saw a giant chick emerge from a giant egg, and sometimes I watched a cork pulled from a cobwebbed bottle labelled 'Emergency', its plume of escaped vapour whirling up and up until it fashioned itself into the shape of a turbaned genie whose blue eyes flashed bolts of lightning. Over and over, as though words could drown the roar of that awful wind, I murmured those lines of Tennyson:

> Oh that 'twere possible
> After long grief and pain
> To find the arms of my true love
> Round me once again.

And I had such regrets, for I'd never known an untrue love, let alone one of the other sort, and the only arms that had ever tenderly held me were those of my mother.

By degrees, I pulled myself together. I think at the beginning we sang to keep our spirits up: hymns, ballads, bits of Evensong. Cherry gallantly tried to warble 'Silver Threads Among the Gold', but when it came to the line, 'Darling I am growing older' his voice trailed away at the realisation there was every possibility such a process was beyond his expectations. I remembered the requirements deemed necessary for the Gold Medal for cadets, and duly bawled them out: 'A cheerful submission to superiors, self-respect and independence of character, kindness and protection to the weak, readiness to forgive offence, desire to conciliate the differences of others, and, above all, fearless devotion to duty and unflinching truthfulness.' At this, triggered by some secret memory of his own, Cherry clutched my arm and began to laugh. Then the roof went. The topmost rocks of the walls fell in upon us, together with a blanket of drift.

The fact that we were almost into our sleeping bags saved us, that and the ridge above us which in some measure deflected the wind howling towards the Ross Sea. Cherry dived forward to help Bill, who shouted, 'See to yourself!' and Cherry still persisting, 'Please, Cherry, please.' All the urgency and worry in the world was in his voice, for he held himself responsible for our ghastly dilemma.

Somehow we burrowed deeper into those wretched bags, pulling them over and round until we lay on that wild mountainside cocooned in ragged shrouds, nothing between us and the hidden stars but that swirling, maddening blizzard.

I think we dozed a good bit; the temperature had risen with the storm, and we were kept almost snug by the snow that fell upon us. Every now and then I kicked out at Cherry to see if he still lived, and all of us heaved up at intervals to jerk the drift away. We didn't eat for two days and two nights, apart from handfuls of snow to ease our raw throats and a boiled sweet apiece in honour of Bill's birthday.

On the Monday there was a lull in the storm. Though it was still blowing we could talk without shouting. We asked each other how we felt ... Pretty well, thank you, all things considered; if Bill's eye was better ... Oh, yes, much better, thank you; if Cherry's hands were on the mend ... Thank you, yes ... The swelling is much reduced. None of us enquired how we were going to survive.

The wind further abating, we got out of our bags and searched for the tent. I don't think any of us really thought we'd find it, but we went through the motions. We were lucky in that all our gear was intact, save for two pieces of the cooker and a pair of Cherry's socks which had been snatched from his finneskö. At last Bill said we must cook ourselves a meal, though it was a curious fact we had little desire for food; our bodies had taken such a beating and we were so diminished from lack of sleep that eating seemed too great an effort. We struggled through the preparations, stretching the ground sheet over us and somehow huddling beneath it, lighting the primus, holding the broken cooker in our hands, waiting an age for the snow to melt. Then, the pemmican beginning to heat and the smell rising, our appetites returned and we gobbled that meaty mess seasoned with penguin feathers, dirt, burnt blubber and reindeer hairs, and voted it the best dinner we'd ever had.

I went out afterwards to look again for the tent, though I imagined by now it had blown half-way to New

Zealand. There was a small glow of light on the horizon, but the sky to the south was heaped with black clouds and I feared another blizzard would soon be on top of us. I was clambering sideways, slithering down the slope below the ridge, when I lost my footing and rolled clear to the bottom, and there, furled like an umbrella, lay the tent.

'Nothing will convince me this is all down to chance,' I told Bill. 'I really believe we've been saved for a purpose.'

'We still have the journey back,' he reminded.

'We'll make it,' I said. 'There's something else God has in store for us, something glorious. I'm sure of it.'

'You may be right,' he said, staring at me gravely, his one good eye so filled with concern I turned my head away.

That night we packed the sledges ready for an early start. Cherry's come a long way since he boarded the Terra Nova unable to say boo to a goose, and we had quite a fierce argument over the gear. Everything we carried was so swollen with frozen moisture that the weights had trebled, and he was for leaving most of it behind. Bill wouldn't hear of it; he said the Owner would never forgive him if we failed to return without every last item. Later, Cherry confided that when the tent blew away he made up his mind to ask Bill for the morphia and put an end to it all. 'My dear chap,' I said, 'he would never have agreed.'

'I believe I did ask him,' he said, 'but he couldn't hear me on account of the wind and you yelling that gibberish about devotion to duty.'

For six days the weather did its worst. Time and again we were forced to make camp as yet another blizzard raged about us. And by now our bags were in such a

157

deplorable condition – we'd stopped bothering to roll them up and simply lashed them, coffin-shaped, onto the sledges – it hardly mattered whether we were in or out of them. As for sleeping, we got most rest on the march, falling into blissful dozes interrupted by our bumping into each other, at which we woke and comically cried out, 'So sorry! Good morning, is everything all right?' We wasted a lot of our conscious hours working out how many years of our life we would give for a long, warm sleep. Cherry thought two, and subsequently changed it to five, but that was when his bag split down the middle.

On the 28th the temperature was -47, and a crimson glow spread across the Barrier Edge. We wouldn't see the sun for another month but already the light was lasting longer and sometimes the sky turned blue. On the 29th, which was my birthday, though I didn't let on, we came in sight of Castle Rock. Cherry whooped with joy, and a piece of his front tooth spat into the snow. The cold had killed off the nerves in his jaw, and whenever he shouted his splintered teeth sprayed out like crumbs.

Two days later we were within five miles of Cape Evans. Over breakfast, a mug of hot water thickened with biscuit and a blob of butter, Bill said, 'I want to thank you for what you've done. I couldn't have found two better companions, and what is more, I never shall.'

Neither Cherry nor I could reply; our hearts were too full for words.

It may be that the purpose of the worst journey in the world had been to collect eggs which might prove a scientific theory, but we'd unravelled a far greater mystery on the way – the missing link between God and man is brotherly love.

*

Bill said we shouldn't go into the hut, not immediately; we ought to put up the tent and sleep outside. I had thought someone might be on the lookout for us, but there was no one in sight; even the dogs ignored our approach. We could hear Handel's *Water Music* on the gramophone. We stood there, trying to shift the harnesses from ourselves, moving like sleep-walkers.

Then the door opened. 'Good God!' somebody called, and caught in a triangle of blinding light we froze, three men encased in ice.

Capt. Lawrence Edward (Titus) Oates
March 1912

I didn't take my sock off because the size of my foot unnerved me. When I last took a peek it was pretty colourful, blotched with red and purple, the skin right up to the ankle shining with that same sort of sweet glaze one sees on rotten meat. Two of my toes were black. I was afraid to remove my sock for fear my toes came with it and we'd all sniff their stink above the smell of that stew in the saucepan. I wish to God I'd listened to Ponting when he said we ought to bring a pistol on with us.

A quarter of an hour ago I begged Bill for a drop of brandy. He refused, giving the tommy-rot excuse it would do my shrunken stomach no good. 'Please believe me, my dear Oates,' he said. 'I'm only thinking of what's best for you.'

He and Bowers still waste an inordinate amount of energy worrying about the welfare of others, whereas my world is no longer large enough to contain anyone but myself. I was trying to get my other boot off and Bill was squatting on his haunches at the cooker, stirring away at the hoosh.

'Do you reckon a man without feet could still ride to hounds?' I asked, and he had the grace to look discomfited. If I hadn't felt so damnably feeble I'd have

161

snatched the bottle from his medical box and to blazes
with his permission.

I caught Scott looking at me. I don't know what he
saw in my eyes, but a moment later he said, 'For pity's
sake, Bill, do as he asks.'

It was a miserly enough measure, yet the effect was
immediate. Such a huge smile tugged at my mouth my
lips cracked afresh and I could taste the trickling blood.

'Get some food into him,' Bill urged, and selfless old
Birdie tried to feed me with a spoon.

'I will lay down my life for Bill,' I said, or something to
that effect. I felt absolutely liberated, like a stone hurled
into the depths, leaping not falling into that shining
abyss where the piebald pony waited ...

*

We shot the remaining ponies when we reached the foot
of the Glacier early in December. We were all pretty
down in the mouth about it, though poor Bowers
showed it the most, his horse being the strongest of the
lot. For my part, I was thankful Scott had changed his
mind yet again and abandoned his damfool notion to
take them up the Glacier. They'd suffered enough; the
surfaces had been uniformly terrible, and towards the
end we'd had to lash them onwards. I think we all felt
the inflicting of such cruelty harmed us almost as much
as the wretched beasts who bore it.

Bill congratulated me on having got them thus far.
'After all,' he observed, 'they were hardly the best
animals money could buy.' He never spoke a truer
word. The motors, for which not enough spares had
been brought and which now lie under drift on the ice
somewhere between Hut Point and Corner Camp had

cost £1000 apiece, the dogs thirty shillings and the ponies a fiver – and I reckon that was a good few bob more than they were worth. Scott thanked me too, if a little stiffly.

We named the depot where we buried them Shambles Camp, which was an apt enough name for it, and not just on account of the ponies. What with our late start, the almost immediate failure of the motors, our inexpertise on skis, 'unexpected' weather conditions and Scott's mistrust of dogs, our journey so far had been a catalogue of disasters and miscalculations. Scott puts it down to 'poor luck'.

I've never known such a man for making mistakes and shifting the blame onto others. If it hadn't always been so damned cold I think one or two of us might have got heated enough to forget he was Leader and resorted to fisticuffs. It was pretty shameful the way he laid into Bowers when the hypsometer got broken. Birdie was frightfully cast down at being given a drubbing in front of the seamen.

'It would seem to me,' I said to Scott, 'that it's something of an oversight we're not carrying a spare one.'

He didn't go for me; nor had he, not since Birdie, Cherry and Crean nearly perished on the sea-ice. He turned on his heel and went muttering off to get words of sympathy from old Bill. In the end I don't know what the fuss was about. We didn't need an instrument to tell us what altitude we'd reached on the Glacier; any fool could tell for himself when he was a quarter way up, then half, and so on.

Another time he got himself into a frightful fizz over the fact that Shackleton had apparently travelled on blue ice, whereas we floundered in drift. There was also that business of his not wanting me to shoot Jehu, not until we'd travelled another twenty miles or so. The animal was dying on its feet, but I was forbidden to despatch it until we'd passed the point at which Shackleton shot his first pony. One would have thought we were racing Shackleton rather than Amundsen.

On New Year's Eve, by which time we had slogged, heaved and crawled some 9000 feet up the Beardmore Glacier, we took a half day's halt for the sledges to be adjusted. Once we reached the summit Birdie assured me it was little more than a hundred and fifty miles to the Pole. I took his word for it. In my opinion, without him we could have been moving sideways, or even backwards, he being the only one who appears to have any sense of direction.

Scott still hadn't told us which three he intended to take with him on the final run. Even Bill didn't know, though he said Scott had asked him which of the three seamen he considered the fittest, Taff Evans, Lashly or Crean. Bill had told him he'd put his money on Lashly.

Birdie was convinced he wouldn't be chosen; he's very naive and simply didn't see that Scott would be in Queer Street without him. Quite apart from his doing the work of three men, he's the only competent astronomical navigator among us, and if he'd been left behind it wouldn't have been so much a question of reaching the Pole as finding it. For my part, I neither expected nor wished to be included. My feet were in a sorry state and I was none too happy about my leg.

It had been Scott's intention to make another march before nightfall, but the work on the sledges took longer than expected. Petty Officer Evans was practically rebuilding them, so we had time on our hands. We sat in the tent drinking tea, and for some reason I was seized with a dreadful bout of homesickness. It was Bill's fault really, rambling on about those bluebell woods he's so fond off. I was only half paying attention to the conversation, because my leg was giving me gyp. I had the oddest sensation my old thigh wound was coming apart, so much so I was pretty frightened of touching the skin in case it was gaping open. When I did get up the courage there was nothing under my fingers save that puckered scar. It was rougher than usual and there were one or two pustules, but we all had those. We hadn't washed for weeks, or changed our clothes, and the hell-hole we were in before we reached the Glacier – Scott dubbed it the Slough of Despond – when for four days we were tent-bound in a blizzard and the temperature rose so high we lay waterlogged in our bags, had wrinkled us like washerwomen. The pain in my leg was a blessing in one way – it stopped me thinking of my wretched feet. I suppose it was the remembrance of my time in hospital, my return to England, the delayed twenty-first birthday party in the grounds of Gestingthorpe that pitched me into thoughts of home.

I must have listened for an hour or more to Bill rhapsodising over his nature study excursions, and a further hour while he and Birdie drivelled on about the Greeks and their notion of tragedy. I can't pretend to know what Bill's getting at when he says the 'joy of being' incorporates a delight in annihilation; not unless he means it's all right for a fellow to break his neck coming off his hunter when clearing an eleven-foot hedgerow.

Scott didn't open his mouth. Nor did Teddy Evans. In Scott's case I don't believe he was out of his depth, rather that he had as little sympathy with the argument as I had. I reckon Bill's whole philosophy is damnably unhealthy. Any man who spends years trying to find out why grouse fall sick of a parasitic disease, and is tickled pink at discovering it's to do with some blob clinging to dew on the bracken, must have a very limited love of life. Dear me! Bill is the sweetest old chap in the world – one just gets a mite tired of his being so depressingly good.

He and Birdie got onto another subject which left me equally in the cold – something to do with the birds of Stymphalos being frightened into the air by the shaking of a bronze rattle.

'No,' said Bill. 'That won't do. They were all shot. And besides, surely they were no bigger than kingfishers?'

'Well,' said Bowers, 'what about Phosphoros, son of the Morning Star, and his wife Alkyone? Weren't they turned into birds which nested on the sea in mid-winter?'

'Halcyon days,' Bill enthused. 'Jolly good try, Birdie.'

In the middle of their smiling at each other in mutual if mysterious, gratification Teddy jumped in with a reminiscence of the time he'd sailed as a junior officer on *The Morning*, the relief ship sent out to rescue the *Discovery* expedition. At this Scott looked fit to boil over, though he held his tongue. Teddy made a good joke – he said the ship was known as 'Joy Cometh in the Morning'. He spoilt it by boasting that he and a chap called Dorley had been given the nickname of the Evanly twins, on account of their winning the two most coveted prizes awarded by the *Worcester*, Dorley snatching the Gold Medal and Teddy the cadetship into the Royal Navy.

'Gosh,' said Bowers, 'how ripping. I tried for the Gold but I hadn't a hope.' At which Scott took out his blessed diary and began to scribble furiously.

Teddy would have gone on if one of the seamen hadn't shouted out for Bill. Apparently Petty Officer Evans had cut his hand working on the sledges. Before he could go outside to see how serious it was Evans bawled, 'It's nothing, Dr Wilson, sir. Nothing at all. Hardly a scratch. Don't you disturb yourself.'

Scott said Evans was a marvel, a blooming marvel. 'You realise,' he told us, 'that building a sledge in these conditions is phenomenal. Nobody's ever done it before.' And no doubt recording the fact, he continued to dash his pencil across the page.

Teddy pulled a face. Whether it signified contempt for the Petty Officer or our Leader is a moot point. Most likely both. The animosity between Scott and Teddy hadn't exactly been hidden. Times without number Bill had stepped in to keep the peace, and Teddy wore himself ragged trying to outdo Scott on the marches – not that it did him much good; the one thing Scott thrives on is competition and he's a formidable opponent. In spite of his nervous temperament – I've never known such a chap for tears – he's tremendously strong. I'd go so far as to say he has more stamina than the lot of us rolled up together, and that includes Bowers. Meares said Scott reminded him of one of those natives who could dance about on hot coals; he reckoned they withstood the pain simply because they couldn't stand the thought of the mind being controlled by the body.

Until we reached the Glacier Teddy was in charge of a dog team, and time and again he romped into camp after us, fresh as a daisy. This really got Scott's goat; he couldn't wait to send the teams back. I can't excuse him for having allowed his dislike of Teddy to fuel his already irrational prejudice against the use of dog transport.

Some argue that Teddy hadn't forgiven Scott for

reinstating the drunken Petty Officer, others that it went deeper and stemmed from the time he had high hopes of leading the Expedition himself. Then there was that bust-up in South Africa between their respective wives, Mrs Evans blubbing because she'd received an invitation to Government House a day later than Mrs Scott, and Mrs Scott rounding on her and shouting she was a silly gubbins for minding.

The following morning at our hotel in Simonstown, Cherry and I were knocked awake at some ungodly hour and summoned downstairs to join Scott and his wife for breakfast. Cherry couldn't eat anything; he had a fearful crush on Mrs S and shredded the bread rolls into crumbs, which he arranged in rows across the cloth and shoved about as though they were dominoes. Scott was effusively genial, which I took for a bad sign. He would keep saying how well I looked.

'I'm amazed to see you're again wearing bootlaces,' Mrs Scott said – she'd taken an interest in my footwear once before.

'It's possibly Sunday,' I rejoined. 'The two often go together.'

'I've come to the conclusion,' she said, digging viciously into her grapefruit, 'that things ought to be considered in pairs.'

'Darling,' said Scott, 'you're spraying me.'

'If it had been up to me,' she burst out, 'I'd have interviewed the wives first.' Apparently she'd had to read a library book to Mrs E for two hours in order to calm her down, and it was a perfectly ghastly book, all about women simpering over their sewing and reaching for the smelling salts every time a man came within ten yards of them.

'I think that was jolly decent of you,' Cherry said,

making sheep's eyes across the table.

'On the contrary,' snapped Scott, 'it was the least she could do, seeing it was her fault Mrs Evans got into such a state in the first place.'

Mrs Scott wasn't at all put out. 'Don't you just hate women?' she asked me, as though she was something quite other.

Things came to a head at a civic reception in New Zealand. Mrs E took it as a personal slight that Scott didn't give her the first dance, and Evans backed her up. Later I learnt from Atkinson there'd been a hullabaloo in the ladies' powder-room. He'd taken a cousin to the ball, who was present when Mrs S and Mrs E began a magnificent battle which lasted fifteen rounds. Mrs Wilson flung herself into the fight after the tenth and there was rumoured to be more blood and hair flying around than you'd find in a Chicago slaughterhouse.

Bill, being Bill, protests that Scott had nothing against Teddy beyond he regarded him as lightweight and something of a slacker. As I tried to warn young Gran, it simply doesn't do to be seen loafing about when Scott has his beady eye on one. A man could march for nine hours, unload the tents, build the snow walls, feed the animals, see to his personal gear, and Scott would still find him something extra to be getting on with. Meares and I got away with it by decamping to the stables; at least there we could lounge in peace.

If it came to it, I'd have to agree that Teddy is lightweight, but I don't suppose any of us will ever forget what a good sport he was during his command of the *Terra Nova*, or the blazing good fun we had those sea nights we sat round the wardroom table, hollering like banshees and laughing until we cried.

'Weren't they good times?' I asked out loud, and they all looked at me. 'I was thinking about home ... Gestingthorpe,' I lied, not wanting to antagonise Scott by reminding him of how little he'd been missed on the voyage out.

'Tell me about it,' he said, closing his notebook and tucking it into the pouch strapped to his chest. 'I saw the photographs you had pinned up in the hut ... it's a fine building.'

'I'm going to make a few improvements when I get back,' I said. 'In fact, they're already in hand ... nothing very ambitious ... a new dressing-room next to my sister's bedroom, some more shelves in the library, extra kennels beyond the stables ... that sort of thing. One day I'd really like to build a swimming-pool ... Trouble is, the best place to put it as regards sunlight would be on the south terrace, and I can't see my mother agreeing to that. I expect I'll have to wait until ...' And here I broke off, because I don't believe I'd ever seriously thought of the possibility of my mother dying. Well, I had, but I'd never linked it to swimming-pools.

'Titus, old chap,' said Bill, ever sensitive, 'when we get home I'd dearly like to meet your mother. You must promise to invite me to tea. I might even do a sketch of the house.'

'There'll be currant cake,' Teddy murmured, and we all laughed.

'You'll get more than tea,' I said. 'My mother's likely to kill the fatted calf. You should have been there on my twenty-first birthday.' And suddenly I wanted to tell them about my mother and my home and all the memories I'd kept bottled up inside me while we dragged those damn sledges mile after mile and my feet froze in my boots.

'I was in hospital in South Africa on my birthday,' I began, 'after I'd copped it in that skirmish with the Boers. I'd lost three stones and was as weak as a kitten. That chap Campbell-Bannerman later accused the army of barbarism in its conduct of the war, but I just did as I was told. In point of fact I was far more alarmed about the proposed reforms – the changing of uniforms, Wolseley's campaign for the abolition of bought commissions, his insistence that promotion should rest on ability rather than seniority. I was young, don't forget, and hidebound, though I did approve of his wanting to break down the barriers between men and "officers and gentlemen", and dub the whole lot soldiers.

'I sailed home on the *Bavarian*, and my mother cried when she saw me so wasted and on crutches. You've never known such a fuss to be made of a fellow. My sister Lilian used to come into my room in the middle of the night and force chicken broth down my gullet. My brother Bryan spent hours poring over jigsaws laid on a tray across my lap, making out he didn't know which piece fitted into the sky. I think he imagined I'd lost my mind along with that three stone in weight. When the weather improved they put me out in the garden on a deckchair and Violet read poetry to me. It was frightful stuff and mostly sent me to sleep. In mid-June, when I was better, they gave me a birthday party to make up for the one I'd missed the previous March.

'It was a magnificent bash. There was a tea for the village children in the schoolhouse, banners and flags all over the place, coconut-shies and a steam-roundabout juddering away in the Long Meadow, and at four o'clock most of the tenants sat down to a dinner in the main barn, my mother, the vicar and the estate manager

171

taking their respective places at the head of the three trestle tables. My mother's a wonderful woman for catching the mood of the moment, for knowing what's suitable. We had quantities of roast beef washed down with nut beer ...' And here I stopped my babbling and swallowed, the very utterance of the word beef filling my mouth with saliva. Dear God, at that moment I would have traded my immortal soul for a mouthful of rump steak smeared with horseradish.

'After we'd eaten the plum pudding,' I continued. 'Jordan, the head keeper, stammered through an address of welcome, followed by the vicar waffling on in praise of gallant young men, myself in particular, and ending up with a baffling comparison between my "bravery" and that Frenchman Becquerel's assertion that atoms, thought for almost a century to be the ultimate units of matter, might contain yet smaller particles. None of us had the faintest idea what he was getting at, though most gave him the benefit of the doubt and assumed he was being complimentary. At any rate, my mother looked as proud as punch, so I sat there smirking and pretending it was just the ticket, when all I actually wanted to do was go and admire my new steeplechaser, an absolute ripper of a brute, black as coal and glossy with it.

'There was a dance later. A limp is a marvellous excuse for getting out of all that waltzing rot, and after doing my duty and taking my mother, my sisters and the vicar's wife once each round the floor I was able to slope off to bed. I would have gone to the stables, but, to tell the truth, I was more done in than I cared to admit.

'I didn't notice the picture right away. I read for a bit, and then Chalmers came in to put on more coals and I asked her why she wasn't at the dance and she said she was going as soon as she'd seen to the fires. I told her she could extinguish the light. I wasn't lying flat, because I was finishing a cigarette, and I blew one of those smoke-rings, an absolute belter, which rose sideways and sailed towards the hearth, drawn by the draught from the chimney. It was then, my gaze following its wobbling lassoo, that I noticed the picture, still in its tarnished green frame, hung on the wall above the mantelshelf. I found out later that my mother had given instructions for it to be removed from the old night nursery only that morning – I told you she was a woman with a remarkable sense of occasion.

'The picture – it was a print – was of Queen Victoria seated side-saddle on a piebald pony, John Brown holding its bridle, taken in the courtyard of Balmoral Castle. It was a very small pony and its rider somewhat stout. One could tell from the expression on the Queen's face that she found the pony restive.

'From the time I could name things the picture had dangled on its cord above the tin soldiers marching along the third shelf in the nursery alcove. I called the pony Boy Charger. Owing to some bulge in the stonework of the wall the picture mostly hung askew. Before going down for her supper my nurse leant on tiptoe against the fireguard and poked it straight with her finger. When I was old enough I shoved it back into place with the handle of my tennis racket.

'Looking at it by firelight, the reflection of the flames licking the glass, it was easy to conjure up the sound of hooves skittering on cobblestones. "Mr Brown," the stout lady said in my dreams, "be so good as to keep Boy Charger under control." "Get away woman," John Brown replied, "ye canna expect me to hold back the dawn." '

After this somewhat embarrassing outburst I fell silent, and might have remained so if Birdie hadn't asked me if I'd done any pig-sticking while in India. I said I had, but much preferred polo, which struck me as the same thing, though without the screaming, at which Scott and Bill looked fit to poop.

'It's all right, Uncle Bill,' said Birdie. 'If you'd seen what pigs get up to in India you'd feel sticking was too good for them. They root about among corpses, you know. I've never eaten a sausage since.'

It was Birdie's mention of India that set me off again; besides it had been a long time since we'd sat around doing nothing. Usually when we halted we either ate and moved on again, or ate and slept, and now we sat idle in that cramped, wind-torn tent, listening to the hiss of the primus and the occasional burst of hammering as the seamen outside reconstructed the sledges.

I told them of the jackal hunts we'd gone on in Mhow, how we blew the horn at six in the morning. '... When the scent was still on the dew and the sun not yet fiery. A sister of one of the adjutants came out with us on several occasions; she was the first woman I'd ever seen riding astride ... I can't say it was an edifying sight. She was present when one of the jugglers came into camp, the time Maltravers made an ass of himself. This juggler was quite famous. With one stroke of his sword he could cut in half a lime fruit balanced on the palm of his assistant's hand. Pinkie Maltravers was convinced it wasn't possible. Thinking to expose the chap as a fake, he held out his own hand and told the juggler to perform the trick again. After studying his palm for some moments the Indian wallah refused. "I thought so," shouted Pinkie triumphantly, only to have the juggler examine his other hand. "I will do it on this one," he said. "What the deuce difference does it make?" demanded Pinkie. At which the juggler explained that his other palm was too hollow in the centre and the sword would most probably take off his thumb. One could tell that Pinkie was in a bit of a funk, but he couldn't very well show the white flag, not with us all watching, and so he closed his eyes and stretched out his arm. The sword flashed down and the lime collapsed neatly in two. Pinkie said he'd had to bite on his tongue not to snatch back his hand at the last moment, and reckoned the beatings he'd got at school had stood him in good stead. The adjutant's sister fainted before the sword fell.'

On and on I babbled, during and long after we'd finished our evening meal, remembering places visited and things past, my days at Eton, my time in Egypt, the colour of the flowers in the borders of my mother's garden, as though my life was one of Bryan's jigsaws and I was determined to fit in all the pieces, until, the hot food making me drowsy and the picture all but complete, I trailed into silence. Whereupon Scott leaned across and, taking hold of my shoulders and shaking me affectionately, exclaimed, 'You funny old thing, Titus, you've quite come out of your shell.' I admit I blushed.

Birdie said later it was the first time he'd ever seen me so at ease in Scott's company, and I believe he was right. I put it down to the fact that with the ponies slaughtered and off my hands, and Meares and Cherry no longer with us, I was forced to make the best of things.

The following morning Teddy's team – Lashly, Crean and Bowers – were told to leave their skis behind and march on foot. On the face of it this seemed a pretty strong indication of their not going on to the Pole, but one never knew with Scott. Teddy looked the picture of misery all day and even Bowers had hardly a word to say for himself. I asked Bill what he thought it meant and he snapped that he was as baffled as the rest of us.

'Surely I won't be included?' I said, and he said, 'Is there any reason why you shouldn't be?' I hadn't told him about my leg.

There was a lot of whispering between Scott and Bill when we camped that night. Bowers's name cropped up several times. I woke in the small hours to see the candle still burning and Scott propped up in his sleeping-bag, scribbling in his notebook.

At dawn, while the rest of us were drinking our tea, he went into the other tent and told its occupants what he'd decided. Imagine our astonishment when he returned and said Bowers would be coming on with us for the last slog. Every detail of that final journey – tent, food, fuel, etc. – had been worked out with four men in mind, and now it would be five!

As for me, my inclusion was so unexpected that I didn't know what to feel. It did cross my mind to tell Scott I wasn't fit, but when I thought of how Teddy Evans and his lot had been manhauling three-hundred miles longer than any of us owing to the breakdown of the motors, and still appeared as keen as mustard, I felt ashamed. It seemed foolish, never mind cowardly, to back out when only ten or eleven days of marching separated us from our goal. I came to the decision that even if I didn't much want to go on for myself, I very much wanted to do so for my regiment. It would be a tremendous feather in the Inniskillings' cap if I made it to the Pole.

I had to write a letter to my mother for Teddy to take with him, telling her I wouldn't be home for another year as we'd almost certainly miss the ship. I said I was feeling very well, perhaps better than anyone else with the exception of Bowers. I didn't want her worrying about me. I asked her to ignore all the unkind comments I'd made about Scott in previous letters, as it was only the cold and the terrible plight of the ponies that had made me sound so scathing and that really he was a good fellow and utterly decent when it came to things that mattered.

I enclosed a list of books I wanted her to send out to the *Terra Nova* at Lyttelton, so that I could study for my major's exam on the voyage home. I knew that would please her. I'm afraid I've always been a fearful dunce, but I did truly feel that the experiences of the last two years had made me altogether steadier and that I was at last ready to apply myself to books and that sort of stuff.

Teddy was awfully cut up at turning back, and Crean wept. I was sorry Lashly wasn't coming with us in place of Taff Evans. None of us, with the exception of Scott, had much time for the Welshman, though he was a splendid worker in the traces and quite the strongest puller among us.

Scott made a gracious speech before we made our farewells, in which he thanked the support party for agreeing to return short-handed and urged them to remember it had been a team effort.

'It may be us four ... five,' he said, hastily correcting himself, 'who will stand at the Pole in a few days' time, but we will never forget that it was you who sent us there.'

Then Teddy called for three cheers and Scott gave the order to start. With what excitement we set off, what optimism! Every time we looked back those three figures were still standing there, waving, turning black and dwindling as the distance widened.

Our hight spirits lasted all of two days, mostly on account of the smooth surfaces and calm weather. Four in the tent had been cramped enough, five was a squeeze and cooking for five took longer than for four, but it didn't matter when the sun was so warm we could stand about outside the tent in perfect comfort.

Then the weather turned bad and we got amongst sastrugi and had to take off our skis and pull on foot – Bowers, of course, was without his the whole time. Scott got into a frightful dither over whether or not we should dump our skis altogether, and no sooner had he made up his mind and we'd done as he ordered and had struggled on another fearful two miles or so, than the surface improved and he had us plodding back to retrieve them. I think we were all weaker than we let on – I know I was – and we simply couldn't afford to be indecisive and fritter away our meagre resources of energy on such manoeuvres. Cold was one thing, and hunger another, and we'd grown callous to both these forms of torture, but it was simply more than flesh could stand when exhaustion was added to the catalogue of pain. Then it mattered terribly that it took an extra half hour to get the food into our stomachs.

Scott, poor devil, seemed genuinely perplexed at this setback. 'I must admit,' he confessed, 'it hadn't occurred to me that cooking for one more would add thirty minutes to preparation time.' For a moment he seemed cast down. Then he said, 'However, I'm sure we'll get used to it.'

In his ruthlessness of purpose he resembled Napoleon, who, when the Alps stood in the way of his armies, cried out, 'There shall be no Alps.' For Scott there was no such word as impossible, or if there was it was listed in a dictionary for fools. In the dreadful circumstances in which we found ourselves, half-starved and almost always frozen, our muscles trembling from the strain of dragging those infernal sledges, I expect his was the only way. To have faltered at this late stage would have been like pulling in one's horse while it was leaping. He spared no one, not even himself, and he drove us on by the sheer force of his will. And then Birdie spotted that black flag.

I suppose for a mile or two we kidded ourselves it might be a sastrugus, but soon we came to sledge tracks and the clear trace of dog paws – dozens of dogs. Amundsen had beaten us to the Pole. We put up the tent right away. It was curious how we each reacted to the realisation that our fearful labours had been for nothing. Birdie was angry; the Norwegians were poor sports, sneaks, not worth bothering about. When the story came to be told our feat of manhauling would be seen as the greater triumph. Bill busied himself making a sketch of the cairn and the flag and hardly opened his mouth. Scott himself was surprisingly philosophical. I think the shock of disappointment was so severe he could scarcely take it on board. He talked about his state of mind before the sailing of the *Terra Nova* from Cardiff, how he'd told his wife he was not quite himself, that there was some cloud hanging over him.

'Kathleen said it would be all right once we were actually on the move ... she was right ... but I can't help thinking it was perhaps too late. If I hadn't been in the grip of such damnable lassitude perhaps the outcome would have been different.'

There was nothing much one could reply to that, and none of us tried, beyond Bill murmuring that we'd achieved what we'd set out to do and at least we could plant the Union Jack at the Pole.

For myself, it was all one, whether we were first or last at that god-forsaken spot. It was obvious that the best team had won.

It was then that Taff Evans began to rock so violently back and forth in his sleeping-bag that we had to hold tight to the cooker for fear he tipped it over. 'For God's sake, man,' cried Scott, thoroughly alarmed, and he tried to restrain him. Taff flung him off so fiercely that Scott fell against the tent pole and jarred his back.

The Welshman was ranting that we'd all be laughing-stocks when we got home, that none of our families would get a penny, that it was all right for the likes of us, but he was done for, finished. 'I won't never get my public house,' he shouted. 'Not now ... no apples in the orchard, no little skiff at the water's edge ... all them bloody dreams turned as rotten as this bloody stump.' And he pulled off his mitt and held out his hand for us to see.

Scott turned as white as a sheet. I think if I'd had enough food in my belly I'd have vomited. Taff's hand was vast and purple and most of his nails had gone. There was a great gash across his knuckles which gaped so wide that the bone showed through. It wasn't so much a hand as some grotesquely swollen fruit about to burst asunder.

Bill took it badly. He blamed himself for not having attended to Taff's wound when he first cut himself rebuilding the sledges. He gave the Petty Officer morphia to ease the pain. It took a long while to take effect and Taff kept up his rocking and his moaning until the tears stood in our eyes and we stuffed our fingers into our ears to drown that dreadful keening.

We marched on the following day and came to the Norwegian flag and tent. They'd left us a note – 'Dear

Captain Scott, As you are probably the first to reach this
area after us, I will ask you kindly to forward this letter to
King Haakon VII. If you can use any of the articles left in
the tent please do not hesitate to do so. With kind
regards. I wish you a safe return. Yours truly, Roald
Amundsen.'

Scott thought it a bit of an insult, but I reckon it was no
more than a wise precaution on Amundsen's part. The
Norwegians had no more certainty than we had of getting safely home.

We marched another two miles to the spot Birdie
calculated to be the exact geographical location of the
Pole. Taff Evans was more or less himself again, though
he moved clumsily and once or twice I swear I heard him
chuckling.

We halted when Birdie gave the word, built a cairn and
stuck the Union Jack on top. We took a photograph of
ourselves; I don't think any of us had the heart to smile.
Then we started for home.

*

I don't know when Taff died ... a week ago, a month. It
was somewhere on the Glacier. I know that the day
before we'd got into a frightful pickle. Scott said it was
our own fault. We'd started in a wretched wind, pulling
on skis in a horrible light that threw fantastic shadows
across the snow. Birdie said he was reminded of a panto-
mime set for *Ali Baba and the Forty Thieves*, all glittering
back-cloths and eerie pockets of stagy darkness. As far as
I could tell the world was a coffin and the lid of the sky
was about to nail me down. It showed up the difference
between us, but then I don't imagine Birdie's feet were in
the first stages of gangrene.

Around lunchtime – not that we had any food – Scott took the fatal course of steering east. I appear to put the blame on Scott, but none of us disputed his command and all of us followed him like lemmings. Truth to tell, I think he was the only one among us capable of making any decisions. Wilson had snow-blindness, Birdie still suffered under the delusion that it would be worldly to thrust himself forward, and Evans had gone soft in the brain. Scott had insisted Bill give him morphia at regular intervals, for pity's sake, and half the time the Welshman was floundering on in a merciful haze of oblivion. He fell a lot, once raising a bump on his head the size of Bill's blessed Emperor penguin eggs.

When we got up the next morning and had crushed half a biscuit each into our mug of hot water, we had one meal remaining in the bags. If we didn't reach the next depot by nightfall we'd go hungry. I'd got past wanting food, unlike Bill and Evans who were always complaining that they were starving. I could understand Evans's dilemma. He had been a great brute of a man, and doubtless he needed more rations than the rest of us, but it was curious to think that slim old Bill, by nature frugal, should suffer the same pangs as that giant of a seaman. I don't know what torments Birdie was undergoing – he was too busy being helpful, taking readings, being a kindly light in a naughty world to let on what he truly felt.

Half an hour from setting off one of Evans's ski shoes came adrift and he had to leave the sledge. 'On, on,' he shouted, waving his good hand in the air. We stopped after two hours and he slowly caught up with us. We'd hardly started again before he dropped out under the same pretence. He asked Birdie for a piece of string. Scott cautioned him not to lag too far behind, and he replied, 'Goodness, that I won't. It's lonely out here. I'll be with you in a jiffy.'

We had our meagre lunch, and still he didn't appear. Alarmed, we went back to look for him. He was on all fours in the snow, his gloves off and his clothes dishevelled. When we approached he barked like a dog. 'Taff,' said Scott, 'what's wrong, man?' but the Welshman didn't reply. We got him to his feet, supporting him on either side, with the intention of walking him back to the tent, but after no more than a few steps he sagged between us and sank to his knees. He said something then about being sorry.

Scott sent Bowers and Wilson back for the sledge. He seemed terribly affected by Evans's condition and, kneeling, cradled him in his arms.

'You have to understand, Titus,' he told me, 'that a man is often a reflection of another.'

I couldn't make head nor tail of that, and kept silent.

'I know you all puzzle over my regard for Evans,' he said, 'but there's nothing very strange in it.'

'The crevasse,' I said. 'You faced death together.'

'No, Titus, nothing so simple.' And here his face crumpled to such an extent I feared he would howl. I turned away, pretending to look for the sledge.

'Titus,' he said, 'did you love your father?'

'Of course,' I replied.

'And I loved mine,' he said. Then he let go of Taff and got to his feet. 'Stay with him,' he ordered. 'I'm going to help the others.'

I tried to make Taff more comfortable, not that it was possible. I buttoned up his coat and thought of trying to put his gloves back on, but the sight of that awful hand unnerved me. Suddenly he stirred and opened his eyes. 'Lois?' he said.

'Help's coming,' I said. 'The Captain's gone for the sledge.'

He murmured something then about cigars and being sorry, and after that he closed his eyes and didn't speak again, not ever.

We got him into the tent and waited for him to die, which he did around noon. Bowers and Scott buried him. Bill was practically blind, and my fingers were useless with frostbite. They had intended to build a cairn over the body, but when it came to it they were too weak so they just scuffed the snow over him.

Bill thinks it was probably that last blow to his head that really did for him, that and the state of his hand. Scott said he'd noticed a deterioration in his character even before he fell.

'He was usually such a strong man,' he said, 'and utterly reliant, never slack, never slipshod in his work. And he understood what one was on about. Yet the day before we got to the Pole he didn't strap the sleeping bags securely enough onto the sledge. If you remember, one went missing and Birdie had to go and look for it.'

It was the first time the Pole had been mentioned since we'd turned back. God knows, we'd all thought about it and what it meant in regard to our home-coming, but none of us had dared to put our thoughts into words for fear of upsetting Scott. I'd had a dream three nights running in which we approached the Pole and, instead of those paw prints in the snow and that black flag, I stumbled across a small cairn with a blue enamel plate on top with a slab of steak lying across it.

'It's a dreadful thing to say,' Scott said, 'and I know you chaps will take it in the spirit in which it's meant, but Taff's death has considerably enhanced our own chances of survival.'

And that was the first time, too, that survival had been mentioned, or rather the notion that we might not get through. There again, we'd all thought about it – I can't imagine I was the only one who realised the food depots were spaced too far apart, and that blizzards and bad surfaces hadn't been sufficiently taken into account.

'He was holding us back,' said Scott. 'He was simply ...' and here he broke off and we all saw the tears welling up in his eyes.

None of us knew how to comfort him, not even stalwart old Bill. During the last few weeks I'd revised my opinion of Scott, though I still couldn't fathom why he had been so stupid as to disregard the overwhelming opinion that dogs were the only form of Antarctic transport. I still thought he was a poor leader of men in the military sense, meaning he hadn't given enough attention to strengths, capacity, terrain, superiority of the enemy, but I had none the less come to recognise his other, more important qualities, not least his ability to put himself in another's shoes. One could see in his eyes, even when he wasn't blubbing, that his heart was too big for his boots. God knows how, but he's managed to surmount his naval training and retain his essential humanity.

I haven't. Well, it's all there, buried within myself, and I kid myself that faced with some terrible dilemma I'll be able to drag it to the surface, that I'll act out of an inborn sense of what is right, but I fear it's not true. I'm too rigid, too encased in rules and codes of behaviour.

I'm not explaining myself very well, but I had suddenly come to comprehend why Bill loved him. Scott is the man Bill would have liked to have been. Scott can't draw to save his life, but he sees things.

'You must have wondered,' Scott said, 'why I cared for Evans.'

'That crevasse,' Bill said.

'Exactly what Titus put it down to,' said Scott. He remained silent for some minutes, now and then dashing the moisture from his eyes. Then he launched into a rambling account of his childhood, his love for his mother, his fear of his father. 'My father was a drunk,' he said. 'It was what one would call an occupational disease, seeing he was the manager of a brewery. I daresay he had other problems to contend with ... the fact that his brothers and sisters were brighter than him, that my mother was a strenuous character. She loved him, yet despised his weaknesses. All through my childhood he alternated between the good father and the bad one. Sometimes he hit us.'

'Con,' said Bill, 'please, there's no need.'

'Once,' Scott said, 'on my mother's birthday he rose up from the dinner-table and hurled the gravy-boat into her lap. Archie and I were on the landing, peering through the banisters. We couldn't see what went on, but we heard that thud and the murmur of disgust that followed. Then my mother came out into the hall, her dress stained with meat juice, her face blank. She looked up and saw me and Archie on the stairs, and waved. I think she wanted to say something, but words failed her.'

'Con,' said Bill, 'please stop.'

'What I could never forgive,' continued Scott, 'was the way he cried afterwards ... the way he grovelled in self-pity ... the way he pleaded for understanding. Taff was an altogether different kettle of fish. He drank because he enjoyed it, not because he wanted to obliterate the moment ... he never once tried to excuse his alcoholic outbursts. He was a strenuous drunk, and for that I admired him.'

It was later that night that I asked Bill if a man without

186

feet could ride to hounds, and Scott ordered him to give me the brandy.

*

Birdie says we've walked, there and back, over 1500 miles, or will have done once we reach Cape Evans. We're now two marches from One Ton Camp, wherever that is, where Cherry and the dogs will be waiting for us.

I no longer care about distances or arrivals. I've passed the point when I can visualise anyone waiting in the drive, not unless they're carrying a bedstead. All I long for is sleep. Yesterday Birdie got it in the neck for saying we'd gone too far east. As navigator he's supposed to know where we're going. It must be a dreadful bind to be responsible for direction. If it was left to me I'd stagger into the moon. The only woman I've ever loved is my mother. This is in response to Bill blethering on last night about his Oriana, who is apparently in accord with his soul. We have only his word for it.

*

I think it's my birthday tomorrow. Last night I showed Bill my left foot. He blenched. Scott saw it too.

'It's all up for me, isn't it? I asked. 'How will it finish? I shouldn't want to end screaming.'

'Nonsense,' said Bill, 'you'll pull through.'

'Stop it,' Scott shouted, 'tell him the truth.'

Poor old Bill pulled a face. One could tell he wanted death to come like a thief in the night.

'I want the morphia,' I said. I knew we had thirty tablets apiece.

'No,' he said. 'It's against my principles.'

'I order you to hand them over, Bill,' Scott said. 'I order you to give every man the means to choose his own time to die.'

There was such a struggle over it that I lost heart. I lay in my bag, hands, feet, nose, hip, rotting to hell. Dozing, I plodded towards the Pole again, towards that blue dish atop the cairn. This time I saw dog prints in the snow.

Bill gave me the morphia, five tablets washed down with tea.

'Pray God I won't wake in the morning,' I said, and sleepily shook hands with Birdie.

What dreams I had! I think the approach of death is possibly heralded by a firework display of days gone by. My mother came to me, bossy, competent, convinced she could nurse my dead feet into life. 'No, Mother,' I said, 'they've gone beyond recall.'

And then she embraced me, and I thought it was her tears that rolled down my cheeks until the pain in my legs jerked me into consciousness, and I realised it was my own eyes that spilled with grief.

I could hear Birdie snoring. There was a little chink of daylight poking through the canvas above Bill's head. In that moment before I struggled upright it came to me that my greatest sin had been that of idleness. I had wasted my days.

Birdie woke when I struggled out of my bag. I put my finger to my lips, enjoining silence. I wanted to kiss him good-bye, but I was too shy.

'I'm just going outside,' I said, 'and may be some time.'

There was a blizzard blowing. I was in my stocking-feet, yet I didn't feel the cold. I had only struggled a few yards, the snow driving against me, when I heard voices. I waved my hand in front of me, as though I was wiping a mirror, and then I saw Boy Charger, skittering backwards and forwards in the drift.

'Be so good as to restrain him, Mr Brown,' a voice said.

'I'm holding back the dawn,' said Mr Brown. 'Captain Oates approaches.'

I only had to crawl a few yards; the pelting snow rained down like music.

'Happy Birthday,' sang the man holding the bridle. And oh, how warm it was.